No One Makes It Alone

By Andrew A. Valdez

D0958747

No One Makes It
ALONE

By Andrew A. Valdez

KELLERpress

Salt Lake City, Utah

Third Edition

ISBN 978-0-615-21107-7

Cover design: Jamie Chipman

Photos: Jack Keller and Joyce P. Valdez

Published by
Keller Press
kellerpress@comcast.net
noonemakesitalone.com

Printed and bound in the United States

Library of Congress Cataloging-in Publication Data

Valdez, Andrew A., 1951 -
No One Makes It Alone - 2006

PREFACE

This is a book based on the memories, experiences and reflections of an old man and a boy. The stories were pieced together many years after events and conversations. I have tried to be true to people but word for word remembrances are impossible after the passage of so much time. In some cases, names and descriptions were changed to protect the privacy of individuals.

Writing this book was a personal catharsis and a promise kept to, "Tell them who helped get you started." I hope Jack is proud.

Andrew A. Valdez

ACKNOWLEDGMENTS

I would like to thank my family, Joyce, my lovely wife, Sophia, Andrew, James and Daniel for your love and for listening to my stories with no end. Thanks to Lois Collins for reading, editing and telling me she enjoyed the book. Last but not least, I would like to thank my mom. She raised four kids with giant hearts by working hard all her life with hope and prayers that were answered.

DEDICATION

This book is dedicated to Joyce, my wife, partner and soulmate. And, to Jack Keller, a guardian angel in disguise.

PART ONE

What first caught my attention were the shoppers veering away from an old man standing a few feet inside the Smith's Food King store entrance. The man was wretched-looking, with a lost gaze. The front of his pants were wet and he reeked of urine. There were sores and scrapes on his cheeks and forehead, making his face look pink. He was probably homeless, maybe panhandling, clearly an untouchable.

Somehow, the man seemed familiar so I stopped to take a closer look. Could that be Jack? I wondered. Geez, that guy looks like an old beat up Jack! I had not seen Jack for years. When I went to his old house looking for him, someone else was living there. The new resident was not interested in my search for Jack and was very unfriendly.

"He's gone," the man told me.

"Where did he go?"

"Don't know."

"Did he die?"

"Who knows?"

"You should know, you're living in his house!"

"All I know is he's gone and this place was a pig's sty."

"Well, who did you buy this house from?" I asked.

"I rent!" he said, slamming the door.

I decided to get a closer look and walked up to the old man. "Jack Keller?" I asked, tentatively. "Is that you? Jack?"

The old man turned and stared at me blankly, searching my face. It seemed as if his mind was rewinding to find long-lost, buried memories. His face then softened as he remembered. It was . . . *The Boy.*

"Well - if it ain't Andy!" he answered. "After all these years . . . it's you, Andy. My God! It *is* you . . . amazing!"

"Jack!" I stammered, "Where have you been? I thought you were dead! You look a mess! You look awful!"

"Thanks!" he interrupted, agitated. "I'm not dead, but I wish the hell I was!"

A store employee and police officer approached.

"Excuse me," the store employee asked, "Do you know this man?"

"Yes, this is my friend, I haven't . . ."

"Well, take him out of here," the employee interrupted. "Or I'll have him arrested. He's been here before. We warned him not to come here and beg. Look at him, he stinks and is chasing the customers away!"

"He wasn't begging," I responded, quickly. "I think he's lost or maybe homeless. So what if he's dirty? He wasn't bothering anyone."

The employee's agitation was now full throttle. He inched closer. "So what? I'll tell you so what!" he was nearly yelling.

The officer stepped between us and politely asked, "Aren't you Judge Valdez . . . Andrew?"

I nodded.

The employee stepped back.

"I'm sorry, sir," the police officer went on. "I didn't recognize you. My apology. Do you need help with your friend?"

"No, thank you," I answered, "we're leaving. I think he can walk. I'll take him outside. We'll leave together." I pulled at Jack's arm, leading out of the store.

"Okay, that's fine, sir. Nice to see you. I hope everything goes okay for you and your friend," the police officer replied.

Jack shuffled slowly. Walking seemed hard for him. He looked dumbfounded, and then loudly asked, "What's going on? Are you some sort of big shot? How come that cop called you sir like that? What's going on with you? Who are you, Frank Sinatra?"

The police officer and store employee watched as we crossed the parking lot to my car. I guess we made an odd couple, I had just come from the court house, dressed in an expensive suit, and Jack wore a pair of urine-soaked trousers with unevenly cut pant legs. He was gesticulating and hollering as we went. The police officer, watchful for my - a judge's safety - eyeballed us until we got to my car. The store employee was just glad to have us out of there.

"Jack, you're a mess," I said, reaching the car. "I need you to sit on this towel, your pants are wet." I grabbed a towel from my tennis bag in the back seat and placed it where Jack would sit.

"I think . . . " he muttered, "I know that! You're starting to repeat yourself! Spare me the agony!"

"Okay, Jack, I'm sorry. Let's go . . . get in. I'll take you home, buy you something to eat. Where do you live?"

"Down the street," he pointed. "Across the street, until they kick me out. That's what they want to do. They're all a bunch of Nazis! They have inspections, you know, but only me. Only me, they inspect. A bunch of Nazis! They want to get me!" Jack was bug-eyed.

Maybe Jack has a few loose marbles in his old age, I thought. Maybe he's delusional. I frantically pressed all the window controls - to air the car out. The stench was suffocating. Jack was oblivious to the odor but I had to fight to keep from gagging.

Jack started in a calmer tone, "Just dumb luck," he repeated to himself a couple of times. "After all these years, running into you again. I thought you were long gone Andy, but here you are all dressed up like some big shot in a fancy car. Amazing . . . just amazing! After all these years, The Boy! I'm sure glad to see you."

PART TWO

They met on a cold October day. It was unusually cold for October in Salt Lake City, more like a winter December. Andy would be eleven-years-old this month. He was selling the evening newspaper on the corner of Second South and Main Street, half a block from the Atlas building where Jack's print shop was located. Jack had noticed the boy several times. At four-thirty in the afternoon, he appeared on the corner wearing a large, two-sided, newspaper saddlebag stuffed front and back with newspapers. He wore the bag like a poncho. The bag almost covered his entire body and seemed too heavy for his small frame. He would stay on the corner until six o'clock, when he would leave to check in at the newspaper office on Regent Street.

Jack was on his way to the Walgreen's Drug Store and Cafeteria across the street for its hamburger steak special. It was almost five-thirty. He stopped at the corner for the light. The boy approached, paper held up so he could see the headlines.

"Paper, Mister?"

Jack held out the folded paper he was carrying. "I've got one. I buy it at noon. For lunch, I buy it."

"Sometime buy one from me," the boy asked. "You never buy a paper from me."

The light changed and Jack hurriedly crossed with the foot traffic. That little kid has some moxie demanding I buy a paper from him, he thought. After dinner he returned to his shop. The boy was gone from the corner.

The winter was a bad one. The snow came early and heavy. The grayish-colored snow piled high on corners, along the curb and even down the center of the streets, forming a dividing barrier. Worst of all, there was a dense, black

19

fog that crept in from the west every evening. About five o'clock the fog rolled-in, like a high black distorted wall, moving swiftly into the city and making it nearly impossible to even see across Main Street.

By eight o'clock, when most of the paperboys walked home, the business district streets were nightmarish. An occasional bus moved with uncertainty along the streets. Standing at the curb, it was impossible to even see their numbers or destinations. From Main Street, Andy and his brother, James, walked west on Second South, towards home. They stuck close to buildings, touching them as if blind, searching for familiar stores and beer joint lights that lined both sides of the street.

On this night there were two other paperboys walking home close to Andy and his brother. Andy wanted to brag to James about how many papers he sold and how much money he made, but he did not want the two boys behind them to hear. David and Carl were mean and they might try to beat them up and take their money. David had jumped Andy before. He caught Andy going home alone once. Usually, the dozens of boys who flocked downtown after school to sell newspapers and shine shoes stuck together to protect themselves from bullies. This was a lesson Andy learned the hard way, after David, pretending to befriend him, knocked him down when no one was around and robbed him.

Tonight, James was with him. James and David were the same age and had known each other since kindergarten. Although James was scrawny, David would not fight or rob kids like him. He picked on younger kids, and bragged about hitting old ladies and snatching their purses as they carried their groceries home. He looked older than his thirteen years - more like a man-child. He was already shaving, drinking and smoking.

With Carl and David behind them, James and Andy knew they had to watch their backs. Because of the fog, they were walking closer to David and Carl than usual. Their walk home took them into the high crime area with its many bars, pool halls and flophouse hotels. This part of town reputedly housed Salt Lake City's red light district.

Carefully, so David and Carl couldn't hear, James asked Andy, "What are you so happy about Andy? It's freezing and dark and you act like this is fun with that big smile. We still have to get past the bars and cross the railroad tracks. We're not safe yet. I can't even see with this crap fog."

"Cuz I'm going to save enough money to buy me some pants in two weeks," Andy answered, proudly.

"Why?"

"I'm sick of patches on my pants!" Andy shot back.

"Screw that! At least our clothes are clean. We ain't trash or on welfare. That's what mom says is important," James said sternly.

"I don't want people making fun of me," Andy whined. "Even my teacher made fun of me. She laughed with the kids who were putting me down."

"That's just teasing, and anyway, screw her and the horse she looks like! We're poor but we're clean. I hate patches, too, but our money goes to mom."

"All the paperboys are poor but they don't have clothes with patches!" shouted Andy.

"Shut up! Don't talk so loud," James warned.

"Those idiots will hear you." He looked over his shoulder at David and Carl. "Quit talking about money, cuz you don't have it anyway," he scolded.

David and Carl suddenly started walking faster. "Hey! How much money dit you chumps make?" shouted David.

"Not much," James lied. "We didn't sell all our papers, too cold."

"Fools! Youse guys are kinder-punks," mocked David, "nuttin but kinder-punks."

Kinder was the last name of a frail, pale-looking boy who was picked on by some of the newspaper boys. The boy and his father sold papers and hustled the streets. Sometimes, Andy saw them foraging for food in garbage cans in the alley behind Lambs Grill Café and the newspaper offices. The father and son supposedly lived in a building with no toilet or bathtub. The boy always smelled like pee and the father had a stale, sour-like alcohol breath. The boy usually clung to his father, trying to keep jerk-boys away from him. When they were mean to him, the father would finally go berserk and scattered the tormentors.

Kinder-punk was a made-up word used - along with other choice swear words - by the paperboys as a put down. Bad mouthing was a sport - until someone got mad and started throwing punches.

David continued, "I sell all my papers an kip all the money."

"Bull," James replied, thinking, what an idiot.

"Bull is yo mama!" retorted David. "I sole all my papers, put a dime in the paper box, took all the papers out and turn them in and told Dewey I ditn't sale none. So, I keep all the money!" He puffed out his chest. "You chumps freeze yo butts for three cents! That's why you fools! Kinder-punks both of you!"

"Just cuz you want to lie and steal, that don't make us fools - that makes you a crook!" shouted James.

"Screw you! I'll beat you up and take your money!" David hollered, then glared at Andy. "And you! I beat you everyday!"

James carried an equalizer in his book bag, a foot long steel pipe. Pulling it out he yelled, "YOU AIN'T TOUCHING HIM OR I'll SMASH YOUR FACE!"

"Yeah!" Andy shouted, "Smash his face!" Andy felt a rush of adrenaline.

"Shut-up Andy!" James warned, holding the pipe up, threatening.

David froze and looked at James. Smiling, he said, "It's too cold to fight . . . you my friend James. I wuz jus jokin, man." He stared intently at them, while circling around them before leaving.

The brothers waited until they thought David and Carl were at least a block ahead before starting home again. They were pumped, feeling victorious - but also worried. Both knew it wasn't over yet. David would get even. It was just a matter of time. It was the expected response in their corner of the world.

"Wow! He backed down," Andy said proudly. "Way to go, man, I thought we were going to get into it good."

"Don't trust him," James warned. "You know how he is, he'll come after you when you're alone. You need to shut up cuz now he knows you hate him - you shouldn't have said nothing. Don't go bragging about this. Don't tell anyone cuz he'll find out and come after you! You might have to stab him now to make him leave you alone; just like they do in reform school."

The paperboys who had done time at the reform school in Ogden, glorified the "stab-them-first rule" right to protect yourself. If you felt someone might come after you or might do you harm, it was okay to stab them first. It was a preemptive strike rule to justify attacking someone without real provocation.

Stab him? Geez, thought Andy, no way. I'm not doing that. Not now, maybe before, but things have changed. David knows James will hit him with a pipe, bash his face in, and back-me-up. James stood up and David backed down. A huge victory. James scared David. I saw it in his face. He froze in his tracks. I'm not a chump now. I have backup and he knows it. My brother threatened him with a weapon . . . that is ten times better, Andy hoped. Forget about that stab him first stuff, I'll just stay away from him - like always - and get me a pipe like James. Besides, I can outrun him if I have to. He can't catch me, he concluded with shaky confidence, I'm too fast.

When the brothers arrived home, their sisters were in bed and their mom, exhausted, was watching television. The flickering picture tube was the only light in the small living room. After working a twelve-hour shift at the candy factory she was "dog tired." She carried a ton of anger at life, especially towards the ex-husband who abandoned her and the four kids. There were times it was just too much and she exploded and unleashed on the kids. But tonight she was just too tired, broke and defeated. Her Spanish bloodline could be traced to the mountain villages of New Mexico where her ancestors settled in 1680, but she was living as if she were a recent immigrant, working long hours for little pay in English-speaking Utah.

They all went to bed tired and drained except for Andy who was still pumped-up and unable to wind down. Things are going good, he thought. Soon no more patches; and, tonight David backed down. That was progress. David still lurked out there but Andy felt safer. Danger in the waiting - as always - but today the bully showed fear. James was a hero. Well, at least today ain't even been for nothing, he concluded, before finally falling asleep.

The next day Andy was on the corner after school. He had no gloves and looked like a small frozen rabbit. Stiff new iron-on patches covered the holes on each pant-leg knee. He was cold. His feet were numb but dry. His fingers were frozen, gripping the newspaper he held against his chest. The bold headlines told the story, "A Spreading War in Indochina," and, "DeGaulle Vows Peace in Algiers."

Some people stopped to read the headlines. Few bought a paper, most just stared blankly at the boy selling papers in this bitter cold weather. Dressed in a hooded sweatshirt under a thin worn parka, he was a skinny kid. Now nearly eleven-years-old, he was a veteran - three years as a street paperboy. Andy looked even younger than he was. He was growing up on his assigned corner: Second South and Main Street, Salt Lake City, Utah, in the shadow of the Mormon Temple.

The Temple and the Church of Jesus Christ of Latter Day Saints headquarters were just two blocks north. Paperboys worked every corner from North Temple Street to

Fourth South and on both Main Street to State Street. They would shout out their paper's name, announcing the evening's final edition, "PAAA—PERRR - DE-SER-ET NEWS NIGHT - FIII-NALL PAPERRRR." Competing paperboys on opposite corners returned the shouts, bellowing above the traffic and downtown noises.

"Paper mister? Paper ma'am?" Andy patiently asked.

The streets were filled but everyone was in a hurry. It was too cold to be out. It was quitting time and the office workers, who filled the tall buildings, poured out onto the sidewalks. The workers joined the shoppers and movie-goers that quickly pushed to their destinations. Andy stood among this scene, considering money matters. Instead of giving all his money to his mom he was going to keep some and save it until he could buy some new Levi's. At a dime a paper, I only make three cents. If I sell all forty of my news-papers I'll have one dollar and twenty cents. I can give mom half and that leaves half - sixty cents - for me. Times that by five, for one week, that makes three dollars. Pants cost six dollars. When the Mormons come this weekend, I can work Saturday and Sunday in the morning and the afternoon, making even more money. If mom let's me do that for just one week, I'll have enough.

The paperboys from the two dailies were told by their boss to work this weekend. The LDS Conference brings hordes of church members downtown. The LDS twice-a-year conference was an early Christmas to the boys selling newspapers. Lots of people meant lots of customers. Everyone would want a paper. All the newspapers and extras would be sold, especially the Deseret News, the church-owned newspaper.

Just thinking about the conference and all the papers he would sell made Andy surge with excitement. He started yelling, hustling his paper. "DE-SERET-NEWS-NIGHT—FIII—NALLL——PAPERRRR!" He had a nice voice. Most of the paperboys did. "Paper, mister?" he asked. "Paper Ma'am?"

Jack bought a paper and the boy recognized him.

"Finally," Andy said, with mock surprise, "you buy a paper from me!"

"I guess you're lucky today. Maybe this is the first of a hundred papers."

The boy was excited, and wondered if the conference had started. "Are you a Mormon?" he asked.

"Yes - Jack Mormon."

"What's your name?"

"Jack."

"Is that really your name?"

"Yes."

"You mean I'll sell hundreds of papers because the Mormons are coming, right?"

"They're here kid, have been for a hundred years - no, what I mean is I'll buy a paper if you're here. I'll buy one every day."

"Oh, you'll be an everyday customer?"

"Yes."

"Your name isn't Jack Mormon, is it?"

"Just call me Jack," he said, amused, walking away.

"See you tomorrow, for sure," called Andy as Jack crossed the street. Neither was aware how this meeting would change their lives forever.

The next afternoon Jack bought a paper, the second of hundreds he would buy from Andy. And, it wasn't long before Andy started hanging out at Jack's print shop, running errands, cleaning up, setting type for the letter press printer and making enough money to gradually quit his corner. He continued to deliver papers to his regular customers at downtown businesses. Andy would rather work at the print shop where he felt safe. It was his escape, a place to go and make some money. When it was slow, he could do his homework. Beats the streets, any day or night, he figured. Standing on that street corner made him feel like an easy target for drunks, mean boys and jerks. He always had to be on the alert, watching.

Jack was fine with the boy latching on more and more. He had no kids and was lonely. The boy had come in from the cold and warmed up the place. Jack couldn't pay a lot but it was enough for Andy to leave his established street corner. Andy made sure of that before he proposed to Jack that he create a job for him.

"I already do a lot around here," Andy told Jack, repeatedly, "so I might as well work here. A couple of hours a day is all I'm asking for."

"Well, there's no free money, so you do need to work. Sometimes, I won't be able to pay you right away. I don't get paid either unless I get a job out. Sometimes I don't get paid right away so we go with nothing." He changed his tone, "This is a business not a clubhouse. You can't have your friends hanging around - just your brother. If I make a list, so you know what to do, you better do it. Get it?"

"Yeah, Jack I get it. You know I can work."

"We'll see . . . And, I want you to play sports. That's hard work, too."

"Why?"

"To get you off the streets. To teach you how to behave, to follow rules, to get along with people."

"I do."

"Sometimes you do, but like everyone else, sometimes you don't."

"What sport?"

"Tennis."

"Why?"

"Because I won a racquet at Lagoon last summer and I know how to play. I can teach you."

"What's that?"

"It's a sport with a racquet and balls."

"No. What's Lagoon?"

"Oh. It's a park with rides and games, I'll take you there some day."

"Will you take me and my brother?"

"You bet, but I want you to go to your school library and look up tennis and read about it. If you learn to play tennis, someday you will go to college."

"Sure, Jack." Andy said, raising an eyebrow.

" I mean it! You might play tennis for a college someday."

"Well, when are you going to bring me the racquet?"

"Tomorrow. But first things first, you go to the library, look up tennis, and tell me what you learn. Then, I'll give you the racquet. Deal?"

"It's a deal, Jack, tomorrow for sure." Andy paused, before continuing, "But, isn't tennis a sissy sport?"

"Yeah?" Jack said, with his hands on his hips. "Tell Pancho Gonzales that."

"Who's that? Where's he from?"

"The same side of the tracks as you, but not your Westside."

"Well, just don't try to turn me into a Mormon. That's what my mom said you'd do."

"Oh?"

"Yeah, I'm a Catholic you know."

"Look, let me tell you something about Mormons. They aren't Martians, they're like everyone else. Catholic's believe that God sometimes has appeared to people, like Moses or Noah. He talked to them, showed them the way. You do know about Noah's Ark, right?"

"Yeah."

"Remember? God told him what he had to do because the floods were coming. He did what he was told, built a ship and gathered all the animals in pairs to save them. Most religions say that God comes in many ways to talk to people at different times. For example, a burning bush or in the form of an animal . . . Well, the Mormons believe God appeared with his son and spoke to a little boy who had been praying for God's help. The boy recorded his words - like a witness statement - and from that came some plates, like a new Bible. The boy told others what God had told him, about the keys to the kingdom of heaven . . . and things people need to do in this life to get to the next life. The boy took what God told him, wrote it down and printed it into a book. The Book of Mormon. The messages weren't new, though. They were in all the old gospels and religious teachings. The messages were to be kind, decent and appreciate others. Be patient and humble, without bragging and help others. Common sense stuff, you know, that people for-get."

"How old was this kid?"

"He was fourteen."

"What's his name?"

"Joseph Smith."

"Geez, that kid wasn't much older than me, just a couple of years. Lucky kid, huh - if he really did get to meet God and all."

"Yes, but he suffered, too. When he was older, those who didn't believe him put hot tar over his body and then spread feathers on him. Some thought he was a kook and treated him bad. But like Noah and others before him, he was strong in his belief. He believed God wanted him to start the Mormon Church in this country to bring all the gospels together as one - and that's what he did. He started the Mormon Church. They finally killed him and his broth-er."

"Geez, Jack . . . I don't think Moses or Noah got killed."

"Well, anyway, tell your mom not to worry. Being a Mormon isn't much different than most other religions, we all believe in a higher being and calling. Acting good and decent to each other is the same in all religions, it's what really matters the most in this life anyway. God is in our hearts, not our skin or what group we belong too. We are all judged by our hearts, not our religion."

"I can't believe they would tar and feather anyone. What a bunch of punks."

"Don't call names, even if you think it. It will just bring more bad thoughts and a bad spirit. Those were hard times to understand, a lot of hatred and a lot of people suffered and were killed.

"But right now you and I got a deal - work, tennis and . . . taking on the world. Whether we are Mormons, Catholic or from the moon, no one makes it alone Andy. No one makes it alone . . . okay?"

"Sure, Jack, anything you say . . . you're the boss. Thanks for the preaching, too."

"Don't be a weisenheimer either or you don't eat tonight!"

"What's that?"

"Forget it, let's go eat."

In the evenings on the free public courts at Liberty Park, Jack gave Andy tennis lessons. He started by standing in front of Andy showing him in slow motion the racquet swing and having him follow without a racquet. He described the forehand stroke as a one-handed batting stroke, to place the ball, not go for the home run. He showed him how to lead with the butt of the racquet - the end of the handle - when swinging at the ball. His teaching technique consisted mostly of yelling with intermittent attempts to do it himself, showing by example. But Jack was not a good player so when this did not bring the right result he changed to being a human ball machine, hitting balls to Andy with corrective instruction on every shot. Calmly, if possible.

"Swing through the ball - don't push it or slap it, follow through it! The racquet head has to follow your wrist. Hit through the ball and finish in front all the way to your left shoulder. Finish your swing high! EYES ON THE BALL! Don't look at the ball . . . WATCH the ball!" he yelled repeatedly. Sometimes he screamed like a man possessed, especially when Andy would blast tennis balls - like a baseball - long and out to the back court fence.

"Hit your forehand flatter . . . compact short swings . . . don't windmill your stroke . . . don't get too close to the ball . . . give yourself space, like a baseball batter, avoid the inside ball by spacing . . . use your feet . . . get in position! racquet back as soon as the ball leaves my racquet. Hit the ball in front of you! Hit through the ball!"

They practiced for hours, the lesson ending only when the lights would abruptly shut off, leaving Andy and Jack in the pitch black, scrambling for tennis balls still scattered over the tennis court.

"Jack, you said you were going to watch the time so we don't have to find our balls in the dark," needled Andy.

"I know - next time Andy. I think the lights go off at different times every night."

"Jack, the only thing going off every night is you. Try not to yell so much, people are looking at us cuz they think you're nuts or something."

" Yeah, yeah - and the cow jumped over the moon. You are getting better. That's my only concern right now. You're doing great."

" I know, Jack. I'm a natural."

Andy picked up the game quickly. He was athletic and could run and change directions like a rabbit. He chased every ball whether hit in or out. He never seemed to get tired and loved to play every day. He argued constantly about scoring, wanting to score his own way: by points one, two, three, four - game. Instead of love, 15, 30, 40, deuce, advantage - game.

"Why not just say zero instead of love?"

"Because that's the way you score."

"How come you jump from zero to 15? That's stupid, you've only played one point."

"Because that's the way you score in tennis."

"Yeah, but it's easier just scoring one point at a time."

"Well tennis is different so learn how to score the right way or people will think you're a dummy. Got it?"

"Yeah, I got it, but when we play, let's do it by points."

"No. We do it the way it's supposed to be done, by the rules of the sport, all the time, practice or play. Don't be stubborn."

"Well, it don't make sense and people who don't play don't understand how to keep score!"

"Look Andy, you have other things to worry about. Tennis is a difficult sport to learn. It is a skill sport, you have to learn about timing, the right stroke, footwork, shifting knees, hips and shoulders and hitting the ball at the right time with the racquet face just right. Focus on those things and don't waste energy on how the game is scored. That's the way things are and that's that!"

"Okay Jack, but I still don't think calling zero love makes sense and it sounds sissy to me."

Every now and then when Andy felt like goading Jack into a debate he would raise his scoring complaint. Although sometimes annoyed, Jack smiled, he enjoyed listening to the boy. He questioned things and had the guts to give his opinion. For better or worse, the boy wanted answers.

The first day of their first tournament was Thursday, June 18. The tournament was titled, the "No Champs," sponsored by the Salt Lake City Tribune newspaper. Jack entered the boy in the twelve and fourteen-year-old singles. The day before on Wednesday they practiced, as much time as Jack could take from his business. They had half an hour on serving, fifteen minutes at the net, an hour on forehand and backhand. It was a miserable practice. The boy couldn't do anything right.

"Relax, Andy. Just take it easy. You're going to do real good. It's just a bunch of kids who don't know much about tennis. That's why it's called, the No Champs. You've got just as good a chance as anyone. Now try this."

He hit a fairly hard forehand to the right corner. Andy ran for it, hit it on the run, and into the net. He threw his racquet after the ball. It sailed into the net, bounced to the hard court.

"I can't do anything right! I can't hit it right!"

"Don't throw the racquet! It's the only one you've got!"

"I don't care!"

Jack walked to the net, picked up the ball and the racquet. He checked it out. A scratch and a dent.

"Let's try it again."

The boy stared angrily away.

"I can't hit it right."

"It takes practice. It takes a lot of practice. This is a tough game. You have to have a lot of practice. Give it time.

You'll do all right. You're a natural. You've got everything - speed, strength, good legs, and guts."

"I hate this game."

"You've only been at it two months. How do you know?"

"I know. I hate it."

Jack tossed the racquet. The boy reached up and caught it.

Andy had small hands and his fingers barely reached around the grip. For an eleven-year-old he was short and underweight. He had good features and dark hair; his eyes appeared almost black, but with a closer look they were brown. He had very large brown eyes, and teeth that were small and perfect. His natural brown skin was darker this time of the year and, by the end of summer, would be a deep bronze.

"Now get back there and I'll hit some to the corners. Run, run. You've got to run and keep the other guy running. Run him to death. Corner to corner. That's the secret. Hit to the left, then the right. Get him off balance. Set him up and then wham it where he isn't."

The boy smiled grimly. "All right. I'll try."

"Great. That's all I ask. You try. That's all I ask. Get in there and try."

Jack hit an easy-one to the right corner. The boy ran over, got it with a good swing and returned it. Jack sliced it so it dropped just over the net. The boy ran quickly forward, smashed in into the corner, far out of Jack's reach.

"Good shot! Great! That's how to do it. I haven't seen anyone do it better than that. Even Pancho couldn't do it better."

The boy laughed.

Jack hit the ball to his backhand. Andy ran for it, swung his racquet back into position, but too late. He lobbed it high into the fence.

"Get your racquet back quick," Jack admonished. "While you're running get your racquet back. Way back. Be ready. When you get to the ball be ready to swing. Okay? Here it comes again."

The Salt Lake Tribune's No Champs tournament began at nine o'clock. They arrived at the Liberty Park Courts a few minutes after eight to give Andy time for a warm-up and to check out the competition.

It was warm and the sky cloudless. The morning sun was bright over the eastern mountains. Later, in the afternoon, it would be hot, an almost-unbearable ninety-eight degrees on the courts.

There the boy was, his first tournament. He was wearing a white tee shirt, white special gym shorts at $1.19, white canvas shoes at $2.95, white sox at $.67 a pair; and, he had two new tennis balls at $.50 each. He was playing with a racquet Jack won playing Fascination at the Lagoon Amusement Park. Andy looked sharp, but he was tired and down. He was in new stiff clothes he didn't like, and unknown to Jack his arms were sore and bruised from punches he received the night before. His mother's friend, an ex-convict, ex-boxer named Fred "playfully" pummeled him while telling the boy to block his closed fist punches "like a man." Andy was secretly hurting - and to make matters worse, Jack had him dressed for gym class in a statewide tennis tournament.

"Well, Andy, this is the start," Jack said, enthusiastically. "Let's hope we go somewhere."

At the small Pro Shop, wallboards were set up to hold sheets of match pairings. At a wooden table with folding chairs, officials took reports of wins and losses, some by telephone from matches played at other city parks. The tournament director, Lee Hammel, a high school teacher and coach, paced back and forth, anxious to make sure everything went as planned. The No Champs tournament was his baby.

The age twelve singles were scheduled for nine. Andy found his name.

"I play Larry Banning. Who's Larry Banning?"

Jack shrugged. "Some kid. No better than you. Don't worry, you'll do all right. What we've got to have is faith."

A few minutes before nine they began arriving.

Cadillacs and Imperials, T-Birds and Lincolns, Mercedes-Benz and Jaguars arrived - and out stepped crisp-clad bronzed boys and girls, loaded with new racquets, with racquet covers emblazoned with their names, most of them blond-haired, blue-eyed and white. Unlike the kids who flailed racquets at Liberty Park, getting little or no instruction, these kids looked like pros. They checked-in at Lee Hammel's table, then swarmed out onto empty courts for warm-up. Twelve and fourteen-year-olds, swinging racquets with great swings, forehands that whistled the ball low over the net, pro-styled backhands, correct form right out of the photos in a tennis manual - private country club players.

Exhibiting superior confidence, they dashed across the courts, crying out, "Good shot!" or, "Watch this serve!"

One said, "Hi, Larry, got an easy match?"

"Sure, some dumb kid I never heard of. This first round is sure a bore."

Andy stared at them.

Jack couldn't believe it. He hurried to Hammel's table. "Who are these kids? This whole bunch? Where did they come from? Are they in the tournament?"

"The club," Hammel responded. "From the tennis club. Pretty good, aren't they? Sure, they're in the tournament. Wouldn't have much of a tournament without them."

"I thought this was just an amateur tournament - A No Champs tournament. Isn't that what it's supposed to be? These kids look like pros to me."

"Oh, it's No Champs all right. You see, a kid who won the twelve year old classification last year has to compete in the fourteens this year. Can't compete in the age group he already won."

"Where the hell does the No Champs come in? I thought this was for kids who never won a tournament."

"I just explained it. If a kid won last year he has to…"

"Sure, sure, I know." Jack interrupted. "Thanks."

Jack turned and walked away. He wanted to hit someone. It wasn't right. He told Andy it would be an even match and the boy would be playing kids with his experience. Now, he had to explain this mad reasoning.

"Gosh, look at those kids play," Andy said. "They sure know how to hit the ball. They all belong to the tennis club."

"How'd you know?"

"I asked this kid here. His name is Lance. He's real good, isn't he? He placed second last year in the twelves.

He's sure good."

"Look Andy. I didn't know it would be like this. I thought it would be a bunch of kids with your experience. I didn't have any idea these tennis club kids would be here."

"It's all right. Maybe I'll learn something. I sure would like to hit that good."

Someday, thought Jack, but not today, that's for sure. "Yeah. Maybe you'll learn something. Maybe we'll both learn something."

At nine, Andy checked in.

"I'm Andy Valdez."

"Banning here?" The man at the table asked.

"I think so. I don't know him."

"Banning! Larry Banning!"

"Yes, sir. Right here."

"You and Valdez on court six."

"Okay, let's go," Banning said.

Andy followed behind. Banning was a tall, slender boy, who was dressed sharp. Wilson, Jack Kramer Autograph, racquet. Cream-color cotton tennis shorts and matching polo shirt and a wrist band.

"Got a ball?"

"Yeah."

"Hope they're better than mine."

"I don't know." Andy held out his balls.

"Only good balls are Wilson Champion. These are dead, no bounce."

"Oh."

"Buy balls that come in pressurized cans. They keep their bounce. They don't go dead as fast. You bought these balls here from Brian I'll bet. Oh well, we'll use mine, played much?"

"I just started this year."

"You've got to belong to the tennis club if you want to get good. Bunch of pansy players here at the park."

"I'm not a pansy. What about getting into the club?"

"You have to join. If they'll let you. My whole family belongs. It costs a lot of money for a family. But you could get yourself in for a hundred dollars."

"Oh."

At the court Banning opened the gate. Two boys were already practicing on the court.

"Hey, guys. We got this court for a match."

"Who you playing, Larry?"

Banning waved his racquet at Andy.

"Him. What's your name?"

"Andy Valdez."

"He's Andy Valdez."

"Hey, Andy. . . "

"What?"

"Beat the hell out of Banning."

"Yeah, Andy. Give it to Banning good."

Geez, who are these guys? Andy thought.

Warming up, Banning hit everything Andy got to him. Andy didn't get many. Banning hit forehands and backhands, lobbed a few, and moved up to the net. Andy had a hard time getting the ball back, most of his shots went into the net.

After five minutes Banning announced, "I'm ready. You?"

"Yeah. I guess so."

"I'll spin for serve," Banning said. "M or W?"

"What?"

"You choose. M or W?"

"I don't know," Andy said.

"See? On the bottom of the handle. The Wilson W. It comes up M or W," the boy said patiently.

Andy thought, it's easier just to flip a coin.

"I'll take the W."

The boy spun his racquet, the head down on the hard surface. It twirled, then toppled over. He picked up the racquet at the middle of the handle, pointed the end toward Andy. "W. You can serve or receive."

"I'll . . . I'll serve."

The boy tossed two balls to Andy. They took positions.

"Want to try a few?"

"Yeah."

Andy tried six. Two went into the net, and four out.

"These go," Andy said, surprised. He tossed up a ball and swung. Way outside. Second ball, into the net. Andy gathered the balls and took position to the left of the center line. First ball into the net. Second ball out, almost to the baseline. Love-30. He got the next first serve in and Banning took a hard swing. The ball sailed straight down the sideline, skimmed the corner and went into the fence before Andy could get to it. Love-40. Andy hit his first serve as hard as he could. Over and in. Banning hit it on the wood and into the net.

"Good serve," Banning shouted. 15-40.

He tried it again. Up with the ball, racquet back, hitting the ball with a swift motion. Net. Not so hard with the second serve. Net.

Banning's game 0-1.

Andy took position, crouching, waiting for the serve. First ball net. Second ball to Andy's backhand. He moved for it, swung hard, too hard. The ball lobbed high and out. Andy was mad at himself. He hit the cement with his racquet.

"Don't lose your temper," Jack coached. Andy frowned in his direction.

The match ended 6-0, 6-1.

The boys shook hands at the net. Banning left to report his victory.

Jack was afraid Andy was going to cry. It hurt like hell when the boy cried.

"You didn't play bad. You got in a lot of good shots. So you learned something. All right. Now what did you learn?"

"I'm not good enough. I can't do anything right. I took one game."

"Listen, you did a lot of good things." Jack's voice was sweet. "Your forehand is terrific. I mean it. You've got a really good swing. Your backhand is terrible - we know that. This kid just had the experience, that's all. Next summer you'll be just as good as he is - as good as all these kids. They have two or three years more experience. They take lessons from experts. You've got to practice twice as hard as them. By next summer you'll catch up."

"I'm thirsty," Andy considered, "let's get a drink. Let's get out of here. I've had enough tennis for today. My arms hurt, too. I hate to lose."

"Go see what time the fourteens' play Saturday."

Jack watched the finish of a match between a

twelve-year-old, obviously from the tennis club, and a boy in denim shorts - even greener than Andy. He was like a lamb. A dazed look filled his eyes as the ball whizzed by out of reach. When he did return it, the ball was out or into the net.

Andy returned.

"Look at this kid," Jack told him. "He plays like he just found his racquet."

"I play at eleven, Saturday."

"If you played that bad," nodding to the boy on the court, "I'd beat you with my belt."

"I must have played that bad. I got beat, too." Twice if you count last night, he thought to himself.

"So. . . ? Pancho's got beat hundreds of times. You've got to lose a lot of times to learn how to win."

"I'm thirsty," Andy said.

"Every day. Practice, practice."

"Sure. Let's get out of here."

"I've got work back at the shop. You go to the show, then come over. Later, we'll come back so you can practice serving and work on your backhand."

Saturday morning at ten o'clock Jack and Andy were back at the Liberty Park courts for the fourteen singles. The second round of the twelve-year-olds was in progress. They recognized some of the players now and the boy who had beaten Andy was again winning, this time against another boy from the club.

"That kid's pretty good," Jack said. "You lost to a tough player. Getting beat by someone good isn't so bad."

"There's the University coach," Andy said. He pointed with his racquet. "Coming down the walk."

Everyone in Salt Lake City tennis knew Warren Trane. Manager of the tennis club, college tennis coach, trainer of champions. Jack read about him often but had no idea what he looked like. He was about Jack's height but much trimmer, wearing gray slacks, white knit shirt, hair crew cut, slightly grayish above his ears. He was in perfect athletic condition. Three men were with him, two younger, probably from the club.

"So that's the big man," Jack said.

"Brian doesn't like him very much."

"Brian runs a shack and calls it a Pro Shop, this guy runs the Tennis Club and the University. You ever hope to get anywhere in tennis in this town, he's the man you've got to get along with."

"I bet he can't play as good as Pancho."

"We don't have to worry about Pancho. Pancho isn't here. This guy is. What's he down here for?"

"Brian said he might be down to check out the tournament. See how the kids are playing."

"I don't want him watching you now."

"I don't either."

"Next year we'll be sure he watches. Well, we've seen the great Warren Trane. He doesn't know us from a tennis ball, but next year he will. And the year after that. One of these days he'll be needing you for his tennis team. He'll know who you are by then, Andy."

"Aw, you're dreaming, Jack." But the boy was obviously pleased.

"I'm going to the backboard and practice," Andy said.

There were fourteen courts at Liberty Park. Three rows of four courts and one row of two. They were constructed during different time periods over many years. First came the two south courts, which must have been set down during pioneer days. Next came four more just north. These six older courts had deteriorated and deep cracks cobwebbed the white cement. Between the old and new courts was a shrub-lined walkway. The first set of newer courts were the best, they had a good playing surface and a dull-colored green that was glare-free on bright days. But the newest courts, and the most scorned, were the red courts. The surface was a pleasant-appearing reddish color, but the surface was rough and uneven. They were hastily constructed by an inexperienced contractor for the National Public Parks Tournament, when Salt Lake City hosted players from all over the country. Overhead lighting hung above the courts but the bulbs would often be broken by an errant lob or from rain hitting the hot oversized bulbs. Players often had to retreat from falling glass and then grab a broom to sweep the glass away.

The red courts had an automatic timer on the lights, turning them on faithfully just after dusk and then off later, close to eleven. The rest of the courts had to be manually switched-on from a locked switch box. This duty fell to the park maintenance crew who sometimes simply forgot. When this happened, there was a great deal of grumbling. Some players threatened to call the mayor or the parks commissioner or the sports editor of the News or somebody. But no one ever did. And when someone finally showed-up to turn the lights on, a great cheer went out. The man would wave and smile, unlock the box and throw the switches. One by one, light flooded the courts and play resumed. Andy liked watching the tennis court lights switch on, there was something magical about it. The deepening dusk was swept away and a new, bright life came to the courts; and, it was fun seeing everyone get back to their game with a renewed enthusiasm. It doesn't take much to make tennis players happy.

It was pleasant at the courts on mild days and in the evening. During midsummer in July and August, the courts were like ovens. Activity almost came to a halt, except for tournament play. If you collapse and die from sunstroke during a tournament, you lose the match. It is a rule of the game.

Andy's match was scheduled at eleven. Lee Hammel called out,"Andy Valdez - Joe Borden, court number twelve."

Joe Borden was a head taller than Andy and much heavier. He greeted Andy casually but seemed bored. As the boys went to the court Jack bought a Coke and watched some of the play on the other courts.

On court twelve Andy and Joe warmed up. Joe had a good swing and a fast serve, but was slow on his feet. Slow or lazy.

Andy spun his racquet and called out, M. He won the serve. He tried a few. They went over fast but only two were in.

Jack watched Joe carefully. He wanted to know what made him better than Andy. He concluded it was mostly experience and practice. Time was what Andy needed. Time to catch up.

47

Andy lost the first set 6-1. The second set he was desperate, running around the court faster than his opponent and getting him off balance often enough to win three games. It was 5-3.

Andy served. He was cautious, trying not to serve too hard. He couldn't afford the ball going out. It was one of many things he had to work on; hitting his first serve too hard and out. This time, his first serve was in. Joe hit it back and ran to the net. Andy got off a high lob to the back court. Joe ran for it, making a wild swing and hitting the ball high and on the wood, sending it straight for the back fence.

To save himself from having to retrieve the ball, Andy caught it in his fist before it passed him - as he had often done in practice.

"My point!" Joe shouted.

"Your point? Whadda ya mean, your point? It would have hit the fence."

"You caught the ball and you were standing inside the line."

"It was going out. I caught it so I wouldn't have to chase it."

"Doesn't matter," Joe protested. "You caught the ball and you were inside the line. Doesn't matter why. You touched the ball inside the line. That's the rules."

Andy glared. He lifted his racquet, as if about to throw it at the boy. He turned to Jack. "Is he right?"

"Of course I'm right!" Joe interrupted. "Don't you know the rules? Why don't you learn the rules if you're going to play this game?"

Jack shrugged. "All right. It sounds logical."

"Dirty playing, I call it," Andy retorted.

"Never mind," Jack answered. "Get in there and beat him. And, don't catch the ball any more."

Andy scowled and grumbled - hitting the court with his racquet.

"Don't bang the racquet on the cement!" Jack yelled. "You break that thing and you'll just be out of luck this tournament."

"All right!" Andy shot back. "All right, already!"

Andy went to the line to serve. He tossed a ball high, swung up at it, down hard, followed through perfectly. The ball whizzed low over the net, dropped to his opponent's forehand, hit closely inside the line, so fast the boy couldn't touch it.

"Ya!" Andy shouted, big smile. Aced him! I'll show this jerk, he said to himself. I'll kill him.

The set ended 6 games to 3 for Joe Borden.

They drove to the print shop without saying a word. Andy was upset about losing. Jack could not think of a thing to say to make him feel better.

At the shop Andy threw his racquet on the table and picked up a cookie box. He turned it upside down, one cookie fell out. "Geez, don't we ever have anything to eat around here?"

"You eat everything we have."

"I'm hungry."

"We'll do some work and then go eat."

"I don't feel like working."

"Me neither."

"What a stupid game! There must be something else I can do better than tennis."

"Okay, I'll tell you something," Jack replied. "If you were in Spain or Mexico you'd probably be a bullfighter. If it was the right time here, you'd be a boxer - but boxing is nothing in Salt Lake City anymore - not since Gene Fullmer was champ. Now it's dead. You go nowhere around here being a prize fighter. Maybe in L. A. but not here."

Jack went on, "What's left? Tennis. What you do in tennis, like bull fighting, is strictly up to you. Nobody in the world can do anything to really help you but yourself. All the coaching and advice and teaching won't mean a damn. The bullfighter, the boxer and the tennis player, they make it on their own. If they've got the guts and the skill - they make it.

"That guy with the sword waiting for the bull, he's on his own. You're out on the court alone. No one can come in to take your place if you're tired or sick or your arm hurts or you twist your ankle or the heat is getting you. It's all yours. Nobody on the bench. You come out a winner - great. Real great. You lose, who cares. You get all the credit. You get all the blame."

"I didn't think of it that way," Andy answered.

"Let's do some work and then go eat. Okay?"

"Okay by me."

Later, Andy piped up, "I'm going to be a good tennis player. I'm going to be real good. Like Pancho. I'm going to practice hard and be real good."

"I believe it, kid," Jack said, smiling. "I know you will."

The final matches of the No Champs Tournament were played Saturday morning. The fourteen and sixteen-year-old boys and girls singles and the twenty-one mixed doubles. At two that afternoon the trophies were presented. Andy and Jack watched with envy, curiosity, and a feeling of determination. All the winners - with smiling faces - lined up holding their trophies and the Salt Lake Tribune's photographer snapped a picture of them. The picture appeared in the Monday afternoon edition, spread across eight columns. Below, in bold type, were every winner's name. The tournament winners posed with their prizes and Andy stared at them with longing. A surge of desire to possess one of those fabulous golden figures, emblazoned with his name overcame him. He felt dizzy and lightheaded. His name, Andy Valdez, would be engraved forever upon one of those trophies, proclaiming him the victor for all mankind to see, for now and eternity. It was his destiny and he could almost taste it.

"I want one of those so bad," Andy admitted.

"Next year, next year," Jack repeated.

To the boy, Andy, next year was a distant star in the never-ending cosmos.

The Deseret News sponsored Public Parks Tournament began June 29. The opening round for younger boys and girls started at ten o'clock Friday morning. This was a ranking tournament, under United States Lawn Tennis Association (USLTA) regulations, and drew contestants from every area of the state. Utah's small towns had little to offer aspiring tennis players, only a few high schools and colleges offered any programs of value. But, players from the tennis club in Salt Lake City always gathered most of the trophies.

Andy cut out an entry-form in the paper and filled it out, entering the twelve and fourteen singles and the twelve doubles with Tom Yates, one of the boys he practiced with at Liberty Park. Tom was a beginner also, but Jack urged them to enter the doubles for the experience. In the Public Parks Tournament they knew what kind of competition they were up against. The naïve hope that upset them in the No Champs tournament was tempered by reality.

Ten days before the tournament the Deseret News ran a series of stories and photos about players who entered. Most of the pictures were taken at the Liberty Park courts. One morning, Andy was practicing with Tom Yates when the photographer showed up and starting shooting pictures of him. He had Andy and Tom do some hitting as he snapped images.

Two days later, Andy was spread across the pages of the Sports page of the Deseret News. It included a two-column wide picture of Andy and Tom, and a three-column wide by six-inch shot of Andy at the net, his racquet hitting the ball right in the center. He was reaching high and on his tiptoes; he looked like the Number One seed making a winning smash.

It was wonderful. For days afterwards, his head was in the clouds and he imagined himself as famous as Pancho Gonzales. The effect on Andy's family, relatives and friends was terrific, too.

"Now they don't think I'm just running around," Andy told Jack confidently. "Now they think I'm doing something really important. Geez, you should have seen my mom when she saw the pictures. She told everybody! It was like a big deal, except for Fred, mom's friend, he just grunted. He thinks tennis is a sissy sport and makes me soft."

"Yeah right, soft," Jack added. "Didn't you tell me that all his kids are locked up? Wasn't he in prison? Been shot, too? What do you expect? His world is pretty small. Nobody thinks tennis is much, though, except those who love it and play in tournaments. Everyone else thinks it's just a big game of ping-pong." Jack shook his head, and smiled, "It's your first year and already you've got your picture on the sports page and a write-up. Better than a mug shot any day."

"That's for sure, Jack! That's for sure!"

Andy practiced hard to prepare for the upcoming tournament. He arrived at the park in the morning and stayed until the lights went off. He pestered everyone to hit tennis balls with him. He mostly practiced with adults. Jack picked him up late, close to eleven o'clock and drove him home. Sometimes, when he finished a printing job early, he showed up to play with Andy or sat quietly and watched.

The morning of the tournament Andy was confident and eager. Thanks to Jack, he now had a Wilson racquet, although slightly used. It was not the best or most expensive model, but it was a Wilson - the kind nearly every kid at the tennis club had. In the twelve's category, he was matched with a boy whose name he didn't know. In the fourteen singles, he had Craig Warren, a boy Andy watched play from the tennis club. In the doubles, Andy and Tom were matched against Craig and Gary Jones. Gary was another club player, not as tough as Craig.

"Just play as good as you can," Jack told him. "I'll watch these guys and maybe I can pick up some pointers on what they're doing right and you're doing wrong."

"I can't think about what the other guy's doing when I'm playing him," Andy said. "Geez, all I can think of is run and hit the ball and hope it goes back over the net and stays in. I don't have time to figure out what the other guy's doing."

"You'll learn how. Just give it time. If I watch, maybe I can help. All right. Go find Tom and get in some warm-up."

After check-in, Andy stepped onto court six with a boy his same size named Billy Johnson. He was obviously not from the tennis club, wearing faded green checked shorts and a yellow knit shirt. Billy was friendly and smiled as they warmed up. He was more erratic than Andy.

Jack arrived just as they started the match. Andy showed Billy how to spin the racquet and choose the M or W for serve.

Andy had first serve. At 30-all in the first game, he took the advantage then readied to serve to win the game. He shot Jack a quick look, then confidently hit the first ball over and in. Billy whammed it into the net.

"Play it easy," Jack said, raising an eyebrow. "Let him make the mistakes. Just steady and cool."

Andy nodded. He took the next game. Billy Johnson had a very wild serve.

Now Andy was 2-0. He hit much too hard and lost his serve, but won the next game.

3-1.

He did everything right. 4-1. Then 5-1.

Jack felt so good he wanted to cheer. Andy smiled like he owned the place. He took position to serve. Up high went the toss, the racquet arching and meeting the ball squarely, over the net just inside the corner.

Ace.

He lost the next point, hitting it into the net. Served a double-fault.

Down 15-30.

A hard serve. Billy hit high and out.

Deuce.

Jack crossed the fingers of both hands and held his breath.

The first serve out.

Second serve in and hit back. Andy took it easily, crosscourt away from his opponent. Andy's point.

Advantage and set point.

Andy took a deep breath, tossed the ball, hit it into the net. The second serve not so hard. Over.

Lobbed back.

Andy waited for it to bounce, hit it easy down the center right to Johnson. The boy tried too hard to put it away. Out by an inch.

Andy's set. 6-1.

The second set was Andy's. 6-3.

Jack watched the boys shake hands. He went with Andy to report the score. It was an important accomplishment. First victory. Really great!

Victory. Tremendous exhilaration. Suddenly, a burst of brilliant blue filled the sky. From the high mountain tops trumpets heralded and echoed Andy's victory over the valley. The world a paradise now.

Andy stood tall before the tournament director's table, "I won. Six-one. Six-three."

"What's your name?"

"Andy Valdez."

"Okay. Six-one, six-three. Congratulations, Valdez."

"Thank you."

"Let's go eat," Andy wanted to celebrate. "I'm hungry now."

"Right," Jack agreed. As they walked to the car, Andy smiled and held his racquet high, waving to the adoring crowd. A band played a triumphant march. Andy could hear it very plainly. But Jack didn't hear the band or see the crowd. All was well in Andy's world. He smiled and waved his racquet at the throng again and they cheered their approval.

They drove uptown to Johnny Quang's, The Polynesian. All you could eat buffet. A very fine place. Not too expensive. A fitting place on victory day.

Andy had never been to a buffet.

"What do I do?"

"Take the plate. Get anything you want. Don't take everything. Just the things you like best. Come back for more if you want."

"Geez, this is great!"

He took potato salad, fried shrimps, fried rice, fried chicken, and egg foo yong for starters.

They carried their plates to a table. Just getting up from a table nearby were people Jack knew, Mike Franchetti and his wife.

"Hi Mike!" Jack said.

"Hi, Jack."

"Hello, Marie."

"Hello, Jack. How are you?"

"Fine, fine. Andy here won his first tennis match this morning. At the Pubic Parks Tournament."

"Hey, that's great," Mike agreed. "Good going, kid."

"Thanks," Andy replied, proud.

"I'm glad you won," Marie said. "Is tennis fun? I don't know much about it."

"How's your boy doing in the Little League?" Jack asked.

"Terrific," Mike said. "He's the littlest kid on the team, but he's right in there all the time."

"It's fun," Andy answered Marie. "But you have to practice a lot."

"Is this your first year?"

"I just started this spring. Jack makes me practice a lot, morning to night."

"Well, it's good for you kids to be interested in something. Keeps you out of mischief."

"I don't have time for anything except working for Jack and practicing tennis."

"Sports for kids take a lot of time," Jack interjected.

"Our youngest boy can't think of anything but baseball, baseball, baseball," Marie responded.

"Well, I've got to get back to the office, Jack." Mike said, shaking Jack hand. "Stop up and see me when you can. I've got some printing."

"I'll be up tomorrow," promised Jack.

"Okay. See both of you."

"Nice to see you, Jack," Marie said, sweetly. "And good luck, Andy."

"Bye, Marie."

"Thank you," Andy said and added, "Boy, I'm hungry."

"They're nice people. I like Mike. I guess he's about as good a friend as I've got."

"He's a real detective, isn't he?"

"Yeah. Private eye. Just like on TV. Only part time job for him, though."

"Does he have a gun?"

"All the time. Shoulder holster."

"Geez!"

The elation of winning disappeared when Andy played his fourteen singles match Saturday morning. He hadn't expected to win, but he had talked himself into thinking a miracle might happen. He might suddenly be playing very good and Craig Warren, his opponent, would have a very bad day. Craig Warren was too steady and too experienced to play that badly. He took Andy 6-1, 6-0. The only game Andy won he earned. Every good play he made came in that one game.

The twelve doubles started Monday morning. Andy and Tom against Craig Warren and Gary Jones. Andy and Tom started out with confidence but everything they tried went wrong. They blew easy shots, lost every serve. Craig and Gary played steady. Although it wasn't always pretty, they just kept hitting the ball back inside. Every shot Andy and Tom made, one of them calmly returned it. The first set ended 6-0.

In the second set, Andy and Tom settled down to the steady game. They took two games. Neither was happy about the beating they took, but Jack was satisfied with the 6-0, 6-2 score.

"Don't ever forget, you learn to play by losing," Jack

reminded Andy.

"You keep saying that!" Andy shot back, hotly. "You keep saying that and it doesn't make any sense at all. I hate to lose. I don't see where I learn anything losing."

"You learn what you're doing wrong and what the other guy is doing right. That's what you learn by losing. Does that make any sense to you, Tom?"

Tom shrugged. "I don't know. I never heard that before."

"Well, let's all go over to the refreshment stand and get something to drink. We'll have a discussion just like the coach and players do after a big game at the stadium."

"Okay by me," Tom said.

"I'm hungry," Andy piped-up.

Tuesday morning as Andy checked in for the second round of the twelves, he stopped at the water fountain for a drink. Two boys walked by and one gave Andy a bad look and remarked to the other, "I've got to play that Spic."

The other boy said, "Sure have to play some freaks at these park tournaments. I hate coming down here."

The comment was loud and intended for Andy to hear. He wasn't sure what to do. Anger and resentment rushed to his head. If it happened downtown or in his neighborhood, he would have been all over them, hitting and kicking.

At the check-in table, the boy stood waiting and intentionally ignored Andy.

"Vanson and Valdez." the official said. "You two on court eight."

Vanson was an inch taller than Andy. Cream blonde.

Self-satisfied. They didn't speak as they walked to court eight. Vanson's friend joined him.

"Let's go up to the club as soon as you're through. How long will you be?"

"Oh, I'll finish this in a hurry. Make it half an hour. This won't take long."

Andy took the far side.

Vanson hit a ball right at him - as hard as he could. Andy moved, swung at it, but not quick enough. It nicked him. Another ball whizzed behind him.

"Hey, kid - you a Mexican or Indian?"

"No, I'm not an Indian."

"Where do you live?"

"By West High."

"A Westside Mexican. I didn't know they played tennis on the Westside."

Andy picked up a ball and bounced it. He hit it as hard as he could. Over the net, low, close to the outside line, a good shot. Vanson turned quickly, racquet flung back, swung at it, picked it up, crosscourt to the corner, touching just inside.

"Hey, kid don't they teach you how to play?"

Andy glared. He wanted to jump over the net and smash in his face with his racquet. That is what he wanted to do. He knew what Jack would do about that. He looked around for Jack - not back yet. Jack would show up any minute and if he caught Andy fighting he might go nuts and not like him any more.

"Hey, you . . . " Vanson motioned to him. "Are you ready? I haven't got all day."

"I'm ready."

60

"You can have first serve. I don't care. Let's get this over with."

Andy tried two. His temper was red hot. He hit too hard. Both out. Vanson picked up the balls, hit them back.

"These go," Andy said.

Vanson took a position, not crouching, standing straight, his racquet held at his side, letting Andy know he didn't expect the ball to be in.

Andy, very mad now, swore to himself and didn't look at the boy. Up with the ball, down hard on it, into the net. Next ball up, a wild, desperate swing. Hard. Over the net, into the corner fast and low. Vanson couldn't move in time to touch it.

"Pretty good," Vanson conceded. "What'd you do? Close your eyes that time?"

Andy made up his mind to follow Vanson after the match until he got away from the courts, then beat the hell out of him. This guy gets a beating.

Jack arrived ten minutes later. Andy waved but he didn't say a thing. He was tightlipped and tense.

Vanson aced him twice. "My game," he proclaimed. "Four-love." He hit the balls to Andy.

Andy picked up the balls close to the back fence.

"What's the matter?" Jack asked, knowing something was wrong.

"Nothing, nothing."

Andy served. He was hitting the ball as hard as he could, but mostly into the net or the far fence.

Jack wanted to tell him to slow down, take his time, but the look on Andy's face warned him not to say anything. He had never seen the boy so upset.

Andy made it ad-out, then deuce, then lost the next two points. 5-0.

Vanson won the final game of the set.

When he had the chance, Jack asked, "What's the trouble? You're playing terrible."

"I know." Andy kicked the fence. "I know it. I hate this game!"

The second set was an exercise in silence. Andy didn't say thank you or good shot or good serve as he usually did. The other boy acted like he was doing Andy a big favor just being on the same court.

Andy took one game. He didn't go to the net to shake hands after the match. The other boy didn't make any gesture, either. He just walked off the court.

Andy kicked the fence.

"What's the problem?"

"Let's go to the shop."

"Want a drink?"

"Let's get out of here."

At the shop after he had calmed down, he told Jack about what happened.

"What do I do? Just let them call me names?"

"For now, that's what you do."

"Any kid downtown talk to me that way, I'd bust him in the mouth."

"Andy, I don't want you fighting on or around the courts. Not ever. That's one thing you don't do. You can't fight anymore - not at school, not at home or the shop. No place, especially on the court." Jacked stressed. "You've got to dress like they tell you and act like they tell you. The club and the USLTA make the rules. They own the game.

"You want to get anywhere in tennis, you go by the rules. You want to go anywhere in life you use your brain, not your fist. That is where your power comes from - intelligence. Not hitting. The prisons are full of people who never learn how to use their brain instead of their fists."

"I hate their rules," Andy answered. "They make stupid rules. I wanted to hit that dumb kid with my racquet. He hit the ball right at me - almost hit me in the face."

"I don't care what he did. If the kids from the tennis club want to act like wild animals, that's their business. I'm sorry for them. But you go strictly by the rules. No fighting."

"I don't have to take it!" Andy said, shaking his head. "What did I do? I didn't do any thing."

"Andy, everybody has to take something they don't like. I had to take four-and-a half-years of the army," Jack recalled. "The first six months was hell on earth for me. Really. I never had such a bad time. I hated the restrictions, hated the routine and hated wearing a uniform. I looked like a million other guys. Getting up at five o'clock, doing everything by the numbers, eating what and when they told me to eat; going to bed when they said, standing in lines forever; riding those damn horses, crawling around in mud like an animal - I hated it. Believe me, Andy, I sure know what it is to do something you hate, and take a bunch of crap from people you wouldn't waste time spitting on."

"The army like that, all the time?"

"At first it was. Then, if you were smart, you'd beat the system." Jack paused, "You know how you do it - beat the system? You laugh at them. Not out loud. To yourself. It's all a big joke. The whole army and the war was just a big

63

joke. A game they were all playing. You go along with their foolishness. You dress up in a costume and make believe all the high and mighties know what they're doing. It isn't forever. For four-and-a half-years I was thinking about the day I'd get out. You see, Andy, you can't tell me anything about doing something you don't like, or acting the way you don't want to act, or being polite when you'd like to bust them all in the mouth."

Andy sat quietly for a long time. Jack moved to the cutter, took some large paper sheets off a shelf and cut them to 8 by 11 for letterhead. The radio played jazz, Artie Shaw's, "Frenesi."

"I remember that," Jack said. "I sure remember that song. We had gone to Frisco for the Fair in 1940. On Treasure Island in the bay. It was wonderful, Andy. The Fair and the new Oakland Bay Bridge. So beautiful you couldn't believe it. And when we got back, that song was one of the big songs of the year. Artie Shaw picked it up in Mexico. He gave up his band and went to Mexico and while he was swimming at the beach, he rescued a girl from drowning."

"You remember a long time ago, Jack."

"It doesn't seem like a long time ago."

"1940 seems like a hundred-years-ago, Jack."

"Yeah, I guess it does. I remember it like it was last month. I got a hell'uva memory, Andy. A lot of things keep grabbing at me, things I wish I could forget. They keep grabbing at me like it was last week."

"I'll be all right, Jack. I won't fight. When that kid said 'Mexican' and 'Indian' he said it like it was something bad. Now, I know why my mom gets so mad when someone calls her that. She says our family has lived here for hundreds of years, even before the pilgrims. Since the time when the Spanish first came and mixed with the Indians. But he tried to make me feel like I wasn't supposed to be here, like I was scum or something, like he was better than me. He's lucky I didn't beat him up. I really felt like it."

"Just beat them at tennis. That's the best way. Laugh at 'em and beat 'em at tennis. That will hurt them most. Hitting people doesn't work Andy, it makes things worse."

Jack's shop was in the rear of the basement of the Atlas Building, a half block west of Main Street on Second South, next to the Capitol Theatre. It was an old building of five stories, with high-ceilings and moderate rent. The basement ran the entire length of the building. Facing the street had been a succession of eating and dancing places, from the stylish The San Francisco, to a series of eateries and teen music dance clubs and even a hippie hangout called, "The Abysse."

The basement contained many rooms of various sizes and most were used as storage for the building owners. One was filled with old rugs and carpets from hotels the building owner operated. Jack's shop had been a storage room. The front entryway was wood frame and wallboard, with a door that hung on two less-than-sturdy hinges. There was a wide hallway in front, and to the left, facing the entrance, a wooden stairway to the first floor. The top half of first floor door was glass and lettered in black, it read PRINTING. Under it was, JACK KELLER, and VARI-TYPING in red lettering under that. On either sides of Jack's shop were storerooms. The storeroom on the north was separated from Jack's shop by a two-by-four frame, covered with chicken-wire. Odds and ends filled the room including tables and chairs and hotels sinks, cabinets, lighting fixtures. The south side storeroom was separated by a sturdy wooden partition.

In the hallway, a window looked out into the alley. There was room to park two small cars.

The front of Jack's shop was painted a grass green and the two-by-four supports were dark green. Jack thumb-tacked a variety of printing samples to a bulletin board. On the door was attached a metal mailbox. At one time, he had a sign with a clock face and moveable hands that said "Back At," but this was stolen and he decided once was enough. Now, he scribbled notes on a pad that was fastened above the lock. Above the door was an awning, striped bright orange and green. Jack's ex-wife added that touch of deco-ration when they opened the shop years before. She painted inside and out and made the awning. Her job included answering the phone, binding print jobs, doing some deliv-ering, and generally helping around the shop. But, in a few months, she tired of the whole business and left him.

A combination lock secured the print shop front door. Anyone wanting to break-in would only have to kick the door and then walk right over it. Inside, a counter ran eight feet long and was four feet high. Sitting atop the counter was an aquarium that Jack and Andy made. Eleven tropical fish lived in the tank, three guppies, four neons, a gourami, two swordtails and a catfish. There were snails too, large and small. While the entrance was professionally painted and the counter with the aquarium was attractive, the rest of the shop was a total mess. Piles and stacks of assorted printing magazines, paper samples, type forms and catalogs sat on top of and underneath odd-sized storage shelves and wooden boxes. There was just enough room to squeeze by the piles to get to a small open space for bindery work and wrapping packages.

Under the counters were shelves with packages of odds and ends of blank paper, old printing magazines, type forms, envelopes, old job tickets, catalogs and a telephone answering machine. It was a Bell Telephone machine that Jack paid $18 per month. Mountain Bell Telegraph. & Telephone charged Jack $15 to install it and then $18 per month to use it. The machine was worth maybe $400 and over five years Jack paid more than $1080 for the use of the machine.

"It doesn't make sense," Andy said after calculating the cost. "How can they do that?"

"They own all the phones," Jack answered with resignation in his voice. "You want a phone, you do it their way. You need a machine like this to answer the phone and take calls when you're not in, you pay what they tell you to pay."

"I think you sure got took."

"Andy, don't I know it. There's your lesson in big business for today."

"If I had a business I wouldn't have one of their crummy phones."

"What would you use?" he asked amused. "Smoke signals? I can see you out in your back yard building a fire and waving a blanket sending me the message you're coming to town. And I'm out in the alley building a fire waving a blanket. Puff - puff - puff - puff - puff. That means Okay, Andy, I got you. Over and out."

Andy laughed and held his sides. "No, Jack. We wouldn't use smoke signals. We'd use short wave radios and call each other on the radio, like the cops do in their cars."

"I'll tell you something, if we were using radios instead of phones, the radios would cost a thousand dollars each."

The machine did serve its purpose. It answered each call with: "Jack Keller Printing. This is a recording. Jack is out right now. If you will leave your name and phone number he will call you as soon as he returns. When you hear the signal, start talking. Thank you."

It then recorded a twenty-second message. If a person talked longer than twenty-seconds the machine hung up. Many customers called again when they had more to say. The machine performed a service but also made some customer's unhappy, speaking into an indifferent piece of machinery.

"Machines are made to only make other machines happy," Jack said.

"How do they do that?"

"I don't really know, Andy. All machines are antagonistic to people. Printing presses hate anyone who makes them work. They smash your finger and break your hand and cut you up every chance they get. Look at the paper cutter. It's sitting there just waiting for a chance to cut my arm off one of these bad days. You've got to look out for machines. You've got to have respect for them. Don't fool around or get careless. They're just waiting for the right time to grab you."

"Aw, Jack, you're just making that up."

At the opposite end of the counter from the aquarium sat a desk. It was something left in the basement by someone who thought he had a knack for woodworking. The desk top was invisible under a six-inch assortment of letters, invoices, envelopes, catalogs, paper samples, job orders, printing publications, Christmas card catalogs, wedding invitation catalogs, notes and memos, photographs, invoices, bills and the new days mail. Next to the desk was a metal stand holding an IBM electric typewriter. It was a much-used standard and Jack didn't know its age. It cost $250. It worked well and could keep well ahead of Jack's typing speed. Andy and his brother, James, often practiced on it - even when they weren't interested in typing. To them, it was a fun machine. The IBM stood up to this pounding. It was strongly built and heavy.

There were two printing presses. One was a huge German-made Heidelberg letter press with a large flywheel, rollers and plates. The other was a Davidson 500 offset printer, one-half the size of the letter press but far more productive. A 25-inch paper cutter sat near the type forms, a scattered pile of slugs, leads and lino slugs.

At the rear of the shop, along the stone foundation, a huge steam pipe brought heat to the building from a nearby plant. Smaller steam pipes attached and crossed the ceiling before disappearing. When the steam was on, the pipes expanded and cracked, banged and acted as if they were alive. The steam pipes were Jack's only source of heat and though the rest of the basement got cold during winter, Jack's shop remained comfortable. Near the heating pipes were more shelves made of the large wooden boxes. They were filled to overflowing, with piles of blank paper of various sizes and colors, type forms, envelopes, magazines,

ιpers and whatever Jack needed a place for. The shop
fire hazard and a one-man sweat shop.

The first to enter the shop reached for the chain
above the counter and turned on the ceiling light. Next, all
eyes went to the floor, searching the concrete for cockroaches. These were of various sizes, the adults averaging an inch,
sometimes more. The invasion of cockroaches took place
long before Jack took-up residence and they are probably
still there. At first, they had annoyed him, as all bugs did,
and he tried several guaranteed insecticides without success.
These were not effective and the smell sickened him.
Nothing seemed to impact these sturdy bugs. After a while,
Jack tried another approach, grabbing a broom and whack-
ing them as hard and as fast as he could. This took a lot of
effort, but eliminated few bugs. It took four to seven whacks
to knockoff a large one. Between whacks, the bugs raced
every-which-way, especially under shelves and tables and
boxes and through cracks in the wall to the safety of the next
room. The easiest, fastest and surest way was to just step on
them. When the light went on, the bugs were momentarily
paralyzed and with quick slapping of both shoes - like a tap
dancer - he managed to eliminate quite a few. He could get
several smaller bugs with one stomp, and one or two of the
larger ones. The biggest cockroaches made a sharp popping
sound as he stomped them. Every morning the dance was
the same, Jack hopping around the room for several minutes. When finished, he used the broom to sweep them up.
He taught Andy and his brother, James, this killing technique. Strangely, with all their fancy footwork, the bug
count remained about the same.

Jack didn't mind the bugs as much as the rat invasion three years before. That winter, for some unknown reason, the basement suddenly swarmed with rats. At night, they ran along the back wall steam pipe as if it was a thoroughfare. Sometimes, they scurried across the floor, at a distance. What he particularly didn't like it when he spotted a tomcat sized-rat meandering along a steam pipe overhead. The rats give Jack a glance and maybe a "Hello" in whatever language rats use. They were not indifferent though, allowing Jack free use of his territory. They promptly got out of his way when he yelled or threw pieces of wood at them.

He complained to the building manager and was assured something was being done. Whatever it was had little result. He often imagined what might happen if they suddenly trapped him in the office and ganged up on him. Luckily, they suddenly disappeared just as quickly as they had arrived. It seemed that the invasion spread to other buildings along the alley and the Board of Health sent out a crew of experts to take care of the situation. Jack never saw another rat in the basement.

So the bugs could be tolerated. At least he didn't have sweaty moments at night thinking about them ganging up on him. He was quite sure he could handle that situation if it ever happened. Rats are something else. The bugs were not friendly at all and invaded his territory whenever they pleased, but they didn't bite.

On July 3, Jack left the shop at four. The Public Parks tournament was in its fifth day and he wanted to see some of the tough, third-round singles matches. Andy had not been around for a few days.

Jack talked with Brian Montrel awhile. He looked over a new shipment of racquets. Some Italian specials Brian was pushing.

Brian Montrel worked for the County Recreation Department summers, and was in charge of the evening tennis court sign-ups at Liberty Park. He had the concession for the pro-shop, which was a sorry-looking wooden hut-like building. In the winter, the windows would all be broken out and then replaced in the spring before the first tournament. There was talk of a fine new club house with lockers and showers for the players. It was a lot of talk. In his shop, Brian displayed new and used racquets, tennis balls, clothing, racquet covers and sweat bands. He also took orders for re-stringing. He did a good job of re-stringing and his prices were fair. He lived close to the park and every day - except Sunday, his church day - he loaded his tennis goods into an old Buick sedan and transported them to the shop. He never left anything at the building when it was not attended.

Brian was a fair player but too inconsistent to make the University team. He gave lessons and encouraged better tennis at the park.

At first, Jack wasn't sure he liked Brian. There were minor conflicts during the first summer between Andy and Brian. Jack insisted some of Brian's prices were too high. The first two years, Jack and Andy were irritated by him. It was only much later that Jack understood how much help Brian had been to Andy. It wasn't that Brain went out of his way to help Andy, but by just being there and keeping the shop open he was a great service to everyone. He kept tennis books and magazines handy for Andy to read. He made the park courts a center for all who wanted competitive play and had nowhere else to find it. He put on a pyramid tournament with trophies for park players and kids who would not otherwise have a chance to ever compete or own a trophy. By all of this and more, Brian contributed to Andy's improvement.

Jack did a lot of grumbling and complaining about Brian. Most likely it was because Brian was quite good natured and he was there every night and handy when Jack needed to grumble. Jack was painfully aware he had a great talent for treating people badly, especially those he cared for. It wasn't that he really wanted to, or took pleasure in it, or that he was ignorant or oblivious to the fact he was doing it. It was a come-and-go compulsion that blinded him to the feelings of others. He treated Brian quite miserably at times, and later he was sorry about it. But, by that time he felt it, it was much too late to say he was sorry.

"Name one first class Italian player," Jack demanded, impatiently.

"Well, let's see," Brain answered, slowly. There are some . . . "

"Just name one."

"I'll look it up."

"You think of one, I'll buy you a Coke."

"How about Scallaretti?"

"He's good?"

Brian laughed, like he was enjoying a private joke. "Sure he's good. He beat Poparino six-0, six-0."

"Who the hell's Poparino?"

"Another Italian."

"You mean, there are really two Italian tennis players?" Jack needled. "And they make all these racquets for

73

them?"

"First class racquets. Good as Wilson."

"Aw, Brian, come off it."

"Really!"

"Okay, you get a Coke."

The Coke machine in back of the pro-shop happened to be in a rare functioning mood. Jack checked out the schedule to see when Rod Smith would play. Smith was one of the tougher University players. He was a gambler and would rather take daring chances in a close match and lose than win an easy one. He was flashy and looked good on the court.

On court number one a 21 singles match was in set two. The match was close, both players serving hard and hitting deeply with powerful swings. It was the kind of tennis Jack enjoyed watching. He walked to the end of the court and watched the serve from there. When the serve was finished he went to the other side to watch the opponent's serve.

Andy leaned against the fence, clutching the fence with both hands.

"Hey, Andy! What are you doing here?"

The boy looked up, not smiling. His face and hands were dirty. There was a deep scratch near his lower lip. Blood was dried on it. His shirt and pants were dirty, a tear in the left side of the shirt. He had bruises on his arms from covering-up to protect his face. Fred attacked him that morning for "mouthing off."

"You look like something the cat dragged in."

"The cat?"

"It's a Norwegian joke."

"My mouth hurts. Don't make me laugh."

"That's what the guy with the arrow in his head said."

"What?" Andy asked, perplexed.

"It only hurts when I laugh."

Andy gazed at the players. He touched the cut on his lip. It was bleeding again. He looked at the blood on his fingers.

Jack handed him a handkerchief, "It's clean."

"My mother didn't have enough money this week. I got in a fight with her and left on my bike. A guy in a green car cut in front of me and hit the front wheel of James' bike. I went rolling onto the side of the road. It blew the tire and bent the wheel. The crazy guy didn't even stop," Andy lied.

"How'd you get the rest of the way?"

"Walked - after I took the bike home. I was hoping maybe you'd be here."

"Man, you must be hungry. When did you eat?"

"Breakfast," he lied, again.

"Come on, let's go to the Jade and get some Chinese food. You can have all the fried rice you want. We'll go to the shop first so you can clean up."

"Let's watch this match first, I can't go home for a while."

"All right, you're not hurt now?"

"Nah, just this scratch. I feel all right."

"With you, there's always something! Never a dull moment. How do you do it?"

"Don't know. It's just the way I was born, I guess. Do I really look like something the cat dragged in?"

"It doesn't matter how you look. You matter. I'm

glad to see you. I'm always glad to see you."

"Jack," Andy started but trailed off.

"Yeah."

"You're the best friend I ever had."

About a mile from Liberty Park Courts, just off Main Street on Ninth South, sat a Chinese-American restaurant, The Jade. It was open late and Jack liked it because it had large booths where he could spread out a newspaper. The service was good and the Egg Foo Yong sandwich for sixty-five-cents was wonderful. Two large pieces of egg foo yong sided by four-half-slices of white bread, covered with a delicious gravy and a large scoop of white rice.

When possible, they took a booth by one of the wide windows. From there, they looked out into the street and watched the traffic. In the winter time, when it was cold and dark, they watched the storms roll in and felt good. It was pleasantly warm and the food was tasty; and, the juke box played good songs. The Jade was filled with laughter from regulars, mostly mechanics, cab drivers, truck drivers and garage men who worked in the neighborhood. The two pin-ball machines in the back corner were Andy's favorite, he liked to play while Jack read the paper and they waited for their order. Jack liked to read while he ate. He said it was good for the digestion. Reading makes you eat slow, he told Andy. This was probably true, Jack had a cast-iron stomach and could eat anything. He ate anything and was rarely sick. So, Andy got the habit of reading while he ate, he liked the comics and the sports section. Jack read the front page first, then the local, sports and the amusement section, He saved the editorial page for last.

They ate and read, feeling content and not caring much whether tomorrow came, and no hurry at all about it.

Sometimes, Jack looked at the boy's face, his dark eyes and his small hands and he told himself, Look at him, don't just read the paper. You can read the paper forever, but this isn't going to last forever. Look at the boy and talk to him. Jack wanted to savor each moment. How long will it be before he's grown and then maybe you'll never see him again? Look at him now and think how fine it is to be with him. You have to look at him and talk to him before it's all gone.

Jack knew all about tomorrow. The tomorrow you wanted never to come. Everything you didn't want somehow managed to come around in a hurry. The boy was with him now, quiet and warm. To the boy, it would be like this forever, only better.

Jack looked at the boy. He wanted to get the picture securely in his mind, so someday he would be able to remember it exactly as it was. He would remember the feeling and how fine it was to be with the boy and watch him grow and help him when he needed help and be needed by him. The best feeling of all was be needed. Without that, you didn't really have anything of value. Without that, your whole time of living didn't mean very much at all.

The Fall Tournament was the last of the year and it was held at the Salt Lake Tennis Club. It began at four o'clock on Thursday, September 17, and would continue through Saturday. It was an important tournament, the last one before the end-of-the-year rankings were announced.

After school Andy rode his bike uptown as fast as he

could. Jack was waiting behind the print shop at his little French car.

Andy threw his books in the back seat.

"I've got to change clothes."

"Change when you get there. We've just got time to make it. I called and said we might be a few minutes late. You know how that Marlon kid is - and his father. His father will be sure to default you after fifteen minutes. Put your bike in the shop. Come on, let's go."

Jack drove to seventh east, past Liberty Park to twenty-first east street. It was the quickest route. They made it in twenty-five minutes. It was ten after four.

"Go change in the locker room. I'll check you in. No time for warm-up. Hope you're playing good today."

"Marlon isn't so tough."

"He doesn't lose very often."

"I'll beat him next year."

"You'll beat them all next year. I wish sometimes this was next year."

"Get my racquet. Have we got any decent balls?"

"You always have to have new balls?"

"The old ones don't bounce good."

"Go change your clothes. I'll buy a couple new Wilsons. Hurry."

Jack took the racquet and walked between the courts to the clubhouse. Boys and girls in neatly pressed white outfits were starting their matches. After the hot summer they were tanned and healthy looking. Tennis kept a kid healthy.

Jack climbed the stairs to the social room and office. It was a pleasant-looking place. On one side were lounge chairs, sofas, a color television, some tables with tennis magazines. On the other side, was a snack bar. From there, through a large glass door, the swimming pool could be seen.

On a bulletin board were the pairings. Jack made a quick check to see who Andy would play in the fourteens. He went over the table where Mrs. Groggin was checking in the players.

"Hello, Mr. Keller. Andy here?" She was a nice person. Always good natured and friendly to Andy. A bit too heavy to be physically active in tennis, but she always helped with the tournaments.

"Yes. Changing clothes. What's the fee?"

"Two dollars for singles. Two dollars for doubles."

Jack put down six dollars. "He's in twelve and fourteen singles and fourteen doubles."

"All right. I've made a note that Andy Valdez is paid. He does have a USLTA card, doesn't he?"

"Yes. When does he need a new one?"

"Not until January."

"Tennis is sure expensive."

Mrs. Groggin smiled. "Isn't it? At our house it's tennis and taxes. Three kids to outfit: clothes and racquets and trips and lessons. But we all love it."

"There are a lot of worse ways to spend your money." Jack, smiled.

"I'm sure there are. But - sometimes I think . . . " She paused, smiled and looked around, as if to make sure no one else was listening. She was about to say something but never said it. Several boys came rushing through the door to check in.

Jack went out to find Andy. He remembered the tennis balls and went back to the office to buy them. Seventy-five-cents each. They looked good, clean white, with soft fibers. A good solid bounce. Nothing like brand new balls for playing.

Andy was on the balcony, looking for Jack.

"What court you on?"

"Six. I'm sure glad it isn't one of these. I'd hate to have all the people from the club watching me."

"Do the best you can, Andy. Play it steady. Don't get excited and don't lose your temper, no fighting."

"I'll try."

"Okay, kid. Go show them."

"You'll come down to the courts?"

"I'll be there."

"I feel better if you're watching. These kids . . . might say something like . . . are you suppose to be here?"

"Yes, don't worry. Go play."

There was a wide balcony on the north side of the building overlooking courts one to three. Metal chairs and round metal tables and wooden benches ran along the railing so spectators could watch the matches, or have a snack and conversation at one of the tables. The club had twelve courts but number one and two, just below the balcony, were the best for watching.

North of the tennis club were the rolling green lawns of a golf course. On the links, players scurried about in orange-colored electric carts. They stopped, decided on a club, sized up the shot, swung the club for awhile, then slashed at the ball. They piled back in the orange-colored electric cart and drove off over a hill. It looked like a pleasant way to spend a few hours.

Past the golf course sitting on the foothills of the Wasatch Mountains sat the University of Utah campus. High up in the mountain canyons were patches of yellow and red fall leaves where the cold fall temperatures had first touched them. After September, snow could come at any time.

But this day was bright and sunny and as warm as any in June and thunderheads were building up on the mountain peaks. It was a great day for tennis.

Jack bought a large Coke and took a seat at the table close to the railing. From there he could watch the play below and listen to the club members. Andy and Jack were the only outsiders. Andy was the only non-club member in the tournament. The only non-white. This must be some kind of breakthrough, Jack thought to himself, though he hadn't given it much thought until that very moment. He looked around the balcony. Mostly women, mothers of kids in the tournament, and a few younger women in the tournament. Men were arriving as they got off work. Scanning the people, he could not see one black face. There were two girls, brown-skinned or just darkly sun-tanned, who may have been ethnic of some sort. Maybe not. Jack couldn't be certain. The black population in Salt Lake City was not large but they were well represented in baseball, basketball and other sports. Apparently, Arthur Ashe's success hadn't reached Utah. Even at the Liberty Park courts, summer came and went and only a handful of black players showed-up. Maybe in Salt Lake City, playing tennis or joining the club was indeed "for whites only," as a park player said to Andy earlier that summer.

Conversations drifted around the balcony.

"What I say is we've got to tighten up the rules

around here. Look at that character out there in the yellow shirt," one person commented.

"That's Dr. Norton - a new member from Beverly Hills."

"I don't care who he is," another voice retorted, "maybe they can wear yellow shirts in Beverly Hills, but we just don't tolerate that in Salt Lake City. Is this a tennis club or just a social organization?"

"I visited the Los Angeles Tennis Club while I was on vacation," the first person responded, "man, do they think they're something. Most of them can't play one bit better than we do, but they sure think they're God's gift to tennis!"

Applause rose up from below for a good play on court one.

Jack went to the end of the balcony and tried to see court six. Andy and the Marlon boy were running about, but after watching for five minutes he had no idea whether Andy was winning or losing. He would have liked to stay put on the balcony where he could sit down, but Andy expected him. Tennis courts are not built for spectators. If you want to watch, you can damn well stand up or bring your own chair.

A fourteen-year-old boy came running up the stairs. "Hey, Jim!" he called out to another boy. "Andy Valdez is beating Bob Marlon." He added, "Three-one for Valdez."

It took a while for this information to be absorbed by Jack. All he had hoped for was that Andy would give the Marlon boy a tough match. Maybe win two or three games. He craned to look. Several boys were watching. Well, this was too good to miss. He hurried down the stairs.

Andy was serving. Jack didn't want to say or do anything to distract him. He stayed back behind two spectators and watched. Andy hit in a fast first serve and took the point.

"What's the score?" Jack quietly asked a boy.

"Valdez four-one."

It was impossible. Andy just wasn't that good.

Andy charged about the court, hitting everything just right and to the far corners away from the Marlon boy, who was trying hard to stop a face-losing defeat.

Jack was afraid to move or do anything to attract Andy's attention. He went back to the balcony. There was a buzz. Marlon's father, a tall man with a Pro tennis player's slimness, questioned a boy about the match. The Marlons were a tennis family and belonged to the club for many years. They had shelves of trophies to prove they knew the game.

"I'll be damned," the father said, to his wife. "He can't lose to that kid. Who the hell is Valdez anyway? Doesn't even belong to the club. He doesn't live around here. I'm going down there and see what's going on."

A twelve-year-old girl ran up the stairs with the news: Andy had taken the first set 6-1.

Jack wasn't prepared for this. He looked down at court six, listening to the talk around him. He went inside and bought another large Coke. Returning, he sat down and looked back to the court where the two boys were playing. Marlon's father was there, probably giving advice, though the rules specified there was to be no coaching during a match. This rule fell to the wayside in a crisis like this. He wanted to go down to courtside and watch - especially if this was going to be the upset of the tournament. He wanted to be there and witness it. It was something he would be able to taste and talk about all winter. But, he was afraid to go. He didn't want to jinx the boy. Whatever Andy was doing, it was one-hundred-percent right. Something had happened. The whimsical irresponsible gods of tennis interfering for a laugh. Something. He didn't want to do anything to change it. He sipped the Coke. He tasted victory, like a liquor spreading through him. Andy had to win. It was his day. Had to win.

"It's 2-0 for Marlon."

Jack's eyes came back into focus.

"It's 3-0 for Marlon."

Jack squeezed the paper cup until the drink spilled out and spread across the table. It dripped down onto the floor and unnoticed onto his slacks.

"4-0 for Marlon."

Didn't matter. Didn't matter. Still another set.

Andy would take it. It was his big day.

"Marlon 5-0."

What was he doing down there? Blowing it now? Way ahead and blowing it? Letting up because he was ahead? Letting up against that Marlon boy who would knock him out of the court if he eased up for five minutes?

"Marlon won the second set 6-0."

Jack rushed down to the court. There would be a break between sets. Andy was talking to some boys. He was laughing and excitedly happy.

Jack didn't know what to say. Dammit! Won a terrific set and then blew the second and there he was laughing like it was just a game and nothing to take seriously and not aware what victory could mean.

"Hi, Jack," Andy greeted him with a big smile.

Jack was in no mood for smiles. "What are you doing? Don't let this guy take this next set. You should have had the last set. You killed him the first set. You just threw that set away. Get out there and finish him off."

The smile evaporated from Andy's face.

"I'm trying, Jack, I'm trying. You said to do the best I could. That's what I'm doing. You didn't say I could beat him. You didn't say I had a chance at all. My arms got sore."

"Take this set. Take this match. We need it, dammit, we need it."

Jack returned to the balcony. If he stayed he would have been unable to keep from shouting advice to Andy. He would be telling him every move. He would be sick with frustration at every bad play.

"Hey, Valdez took the first game in the third set."

Jack relaxed. This was going to be the day. The last tournament of the year. This was what they needed to carry them until spring.

"Marlon took the second game."

It's all right, Jack muttered to himself. It's all right.

Marlon 2-1.

Marlon 3-1.

Marlon 3-2.

Marlon 5-3.

Marlon 5-4.

Where was the prayer wheel? Where did you burn the incense? Light a candle. Light three candles. A hundred candles. Listen to me. Ask what you will. I will do it. I will do it. Anything. Anything you ask. Just this once. And strike me dead if I don't do what you ask, only now let him let him

. . . let him . . .

"Marlon set and match. 6-4."

A satisfied murmur rippled about the balcony and clubhouse.

After a while Jack went to find Andy. The Marlon boy and his father came up the walk, talking, laughing, the man's arm around his son with satisfaction.

He found Andy at the car waiting. He unlocked the doors and got in, not saying a word.

"I don't see why you're so mad," Andy said. "I did the best I could. You told me I wouldn't win. You said he was too tough for me."

"Yeah, I know."

It was a silent drive to the boy's house.

"You're still mad. I don't see why you're mad. I beat him good one set."

"I know."

He took his clothes and books and his racquet and got out of the car. "I tried hard, Jack. I really tried hard. I had that first set and I was sure I'd take him. He was just too tough. Next year I'll take him. I'll take him good next year."

Jack had to say something. He couldn't leave it like this.

"It's all right, Andy. It doesn't have anything to do with you or the match. You did good. Better than I expected. It's just . . . that damn club. It just got to me. After the first set, I started chewing on how great it would be."

"Oh," Andy said.

"I'll see you tomorrow."

"Okay Jack, for sure. See you tomorrow."

Jack drove off. It was absolutely ridiculous, taking

the game so seriously. Building it up to a life-and-death matter. Tomorrow he was going to have to make it up to the boy. Do something nice for him. Buy him something he really wanted. He felt miserable as hell.

Andy's little sister opened the door.

"Hi, Kathy."

"Andy!"

Kathy was eight and the happiest looking kid around. Jack said she reminded him of an old 1930s saying, "Cute as a Bug's Ear." The Valdez house was small with two tiny bedrooms for five people, not counting Fred, who hung around a lot lately. The front room and kitchen made the place slightly bigger than a small apartment. It was located in the heart of Salt Lake City's westside, off 800 West and 200 North. Andy's big sister, Lucy, appeared from the kitchen. Lucy was thirteen and very pretty. She was responsible for taking care of Kathy. Lucy rarely left the house except to go to school and church. She was protective and parental.

"Fun day?" Lucy asked.

"Yeah, I almost beat this really good player. Everyone was watching. But I lost."

"Too bad, so sad," she joked.

"Yeah, Jack got real mad."

"Why?"

"Cuz I lost."

"Oh, brother! What's his problem? Man, at least you're doing something, not just running around stealing and sniffing glue like most of the losers around here!"

"Yeah."

"That makes me mad!"

"Okay, Lucy."

"Jack's lucky you even go with him to play that sissy game with those weirdos."

"Anything to eat?"

"Just some onions I fried."

"Too bad you lost, but you tried. Don't feel bad."

"I'll beat them all some day, that's what Jack says, too."

"Even if you don't, Andy, you'll still be okay. No matter what Jack says and . . . I'll tell him that to his face!"

"No, Lucy, it's okay. After a while he calms down."

"Well, he better. He's lucky you give him the time of day."

They were back at the tennis club Friday for Andy's fourteen single match with Larry Banning. Banning beat him in his first tournament in June. He liked playing Larry. He was friendly and offered a "Good shot" every time Andy hit a decent return. He somehow made Andy feel he had a right to play at the club.

Banning won 6-1, 6-2.

After the match, Larry asked, "Hey, Andy, you in the doubles?"

"I don't know. I was going to play with Tom but he can't make it."

"My partner's parents went out of town. He had to go with them. Want to play?"

"I'm not good enough. I can't win anybody up here."

"You sure had Marlon scared yesterday. He made all kinds of excuses. Said he was just fooling around the first set. He wasn't fooling. You really beat him. He was scared you were going to win. I wish you had. He thinks he's great. I don't care if we don't win. If I don't play I can't win anyhow. How about it?"

"Okay, for sure," Andy said.

"All right then. Tomorrow morning at ten."

"I'll be here."

From the balcony, Jack watched their match.

"Oh, Keller."

"Hello, Mrs. Banning."

"I just wanted to tell you how fine I think it is of you to bring Andy here to play. He's certainly improved since the first tournament. I know what a struggle it is to keep a boy interested and practicing."

"Thank you. Your boys are certainly playing well this tournament."

"I hope you can keep Andy playing the game. He's got a lot of ability. Keep him practicing. Don't get discouraged by the talk. We want him to keep playing."

"I'm going to try, Mrs. Banning. I'm sure going to try," he repeated. "What talk?"

"I guess we'll be seeing you and Andy next spring."

"We'll be there. I'll have him out practicing every day we have a dry court." Jack was fishing for an invitation to play indoors. "And, thank you, Mrs. Banning. I'll tell Andy what you said. It will encourage him."

Mrs. Banning was a fine-looking woman. She had two sons, Larry who was twelve and Dick fourteen. Her husband was some sort of engineer. She had light brown hair and brown eyes and a good solid figure. She had a smile Jack liked. When he saw her at the tournaments he had watched to see her smile. There was a warmth about her. Perhaps she was very rich and lived high on the east side in a very large expensive house and drove a Cadillac coupe.

What talk, Jack wondered? The boy was playing better and getting noticed, and so far he hadn't hit anyone. People can talk all they want, he concluded, we'll be fine.

"Hi, Jack," Andy greeted him. "Larry Banning wants me to be in the doubles with him tomorrow."

"You want to?"

"I guess so. He said it doesn't matter if we don't win."

"You could learn a lot playing with that kid. As long as he doesn't get mad if you can't keep up."

"He won't. He doesn't get mad at anything."

"I wish I could say that," Jack paused. "I'm happy about the way you played today. Mrs. Banning said you sure have improved this summer. She thinks you have a lot of ability."

"She did?" Andy beamed. "I like her, too. She's nice."

"Yes, she's nice. A very nice person."

The Saturday morning the fourteen doubles had them matched against Bob Marlon and Bill Vanson on number two court. Andy was nervous during the warm-up and flubbed most of his shots. The balcony was filled and Andy was sure they were all keeping an eye on him. Larry encouraged him, telling him the best way they should play.

"Give Vanson everything," Larry offered. "He thinks this is going to be easy as cream cheese. When he gets too confident he makes a lot of mistakes. You just give it to him and play back. I'll cover the net, you take the back court. Okay, Andy?"

"Yeah, okay. I'll try."

Banning stayed cool and covered as much of the court as he could. Andy let him have the hard plays. Vanson and Marlon hit everything they could to Andy. He tried but couldn't get back enough good shots to keep them from losing the first set, 6-3.

The second set Warren Trane, the club manager, came from the office to watch. Andy and Larry were down 1-3. The next game, Andy made some good returns from the back court. Larry put away everything that came to him. They won that one.

Trane strolled over to Jack. "Hello, I'm Warren Trane." He held out his hand.

"Very glad to meet you. I'm Jack Keller."

"That your boy?"

"I'm a friend of the family. I've been sponsoring him. Getting him to the tournaments and to practice."

"How long has he been playing?"

"Started this summer."

"Not bad, for that little time. Could use some good lessons. Bring him here next summer. Maybe we can help him."

"I sure will, Mr. Trane. I appreciate your interest. We need all the help we can get."

"Practice, that's the big thing. Practice, practice, practice. It never ends. Tell him I said to keep at it."

"Thanks. You bet."

Andy and Larry lost the set 6-3. Larry was kidding Andy about something he had done in the match when Jack arrived. Larry didn't seem to be upset about losing.

"Hi, Jack," Andy said, watching carefully to see his reaction.

"You guys played real good," Jack offered, then turned to Larry. "You sure helped Andy to stay in there."

"Aw, it was fun," Larry smiled widely. "Andy always tries hard, anyway. Next year we'll beat them."

"Sure enough," Jack said.

Driving home Jack told Andy what Warren Trane said. "You came out pretty good this tournament."

"Except for the first day."

"Oh," Jack said, embarrassed. "I just got upset. I'll have those days again, Andy. You'll just have to put up with me."

Andy looked at him, then away. "Jack, sometimes it ain't easy."

The alley between the Atlas Building and the Capitol Theatre ran straight north halfway through the block, then made an abrupt ninety degree left turn. The buildings were tall and close together so the alley was always in shadow, except for about an hour when the sun was directly overhead. At its beginning, the alley was level for a short distance, then slopped down sharply before leveling off for about ten yards, then it rose at a steep climb before leveling out again. It was like a narrow street in Naples or Florence, Italy - but without the strings of laundry overhead. Swarms of pigeons circled above, sometimes diving and wheeling between the buildings, and stray dogs and cats searched for food. Sometimes at night, small rats scurrying out of dark places. Occasionally, a wino ended up in one of the doorways of the alley, not having the money for the cheap flop-house hotels across the street. At night, Andy darted through the alley at full speed - unless he was with Jack. He wanted to be a fast moving target in case someone tried to snatch him or a drunk tried to talk to him.

During summer cloudbursts, the flat roofed build-ings drained into the alley, flooding it. The water seeped under the doorways and into the Atlas Building. Sometimes it reached into Jack's shop. It was like a streaming current, spreading through the basement. Jack's shop was lucky to be in a higher level of the basement, but sometimes the muddy water was ankle deep.

On the opposite side of the alley was the side exit of the Capitol Theatre and then further down the stage door. There were two theatres on the alley, the Capitol and the Utah. The Utah Theatres' entrance was on Main Street. It had been touted as the million dollar theatre of the Utah cir-cuit, featuring the best acts on the road. As a child, Jack saw Harry Houdini make an elephant disappear there. The Capitol Theatre had also been a vaudeville house and show-cased a very large stage. Now, about twice a year, a travel-ing New York production appeared at the Capitol for a few days. When a show moved in or out, the narrow alley was utter confusion with crates and stage sets and lights and actors coming and going.

The crates of equipment were unloaded day and night along the alley and the space by the Atlas Building basement entrance. Stacks of large crates labeled Lights, Act I, Scene I, Act II Wardrobe, Electrician stood everywhere. In September, "My Fair Lady," arrived with its enormous amount of stage props. The alley was frantic with the stagehands moving equipment and local trucks trying to get through for deliveries.

Through the open side doors, Jack and Andy watched. As soon as two revolving stages were in place, rehearsals began. It was a ballet scene. The male dancers gracefully lifted the girls overhead.

"Geez, look at the muscles on those guys," Andy commented.

"Takes a lot of strength to do that and make it look easy."

"I thought ballet dancers were soft."

"You've only seen them on TV."

The men dancers whirled about, took a few steps, turned and held out a hand. The ballerina's came running and leaped. The men caught them as if they were humming birds.

"They make it look so easy," Andy said, amazed. "They don't look like sissies at all."

Backstage the electricians and carpenters were putting together Act I, Scene I for the next evening's opening.

For a week, with matinees on Wednesday and Saturday, the lovely music drifted through the alley. It was best at night. On a few warm evenings, the side doors in the balcony were opened for ventilation and the singing spilled out, filling the alley. One evening it was so warm they opened the main floor side doors and Jack and Andy watched the "*On the Street Where You Live*," scene from the alley. It was a fine, exciting week having the famous show from New York so close by. Taxis arrived in the alley before each performance bringing the actors and actresses, the dancers and musicians to the stage door.

"They sure know how to put on a show in New York," Andy said, shaking his head. "You don't see anything like this in a movie."

The first news flash on the radio was at 6:25 p.m. Jack shut off the press, pulled the switch, grabbed his jacket and turned off the lights. Andy was due back from a delivery any minute. He waited out by the car, looking up the alley for the boy. The sun set earlier and the Capitol Theatre lights were on.

The boy rounded the corner on his bike and came down the alley to the car.

"Hurry! Hurry!" Jack said, frantically. "Put your bike inside and pull the door shut. Quick!"

"What's the matter?"

"A plane crash out at the airport. Just got the news flash. Let's go."

Andy ran his bike to the basement.

Jack had the car started and waiting. The boy jumped in and Jack gunned the motor down the alley, stopping for the sidewalk, then out into the street.

"Big jet cracked up," Jack announced. "Just happened half an hour ago. This is something for you to see."

"Ever see a plane crash, Jack?"

"Small ones. No big planes."

They traveled west on Second South, across the railroad tracks.

"We can get there this way. North Temple street will be blocked. We can go this way past Redwood Road and then turn to the airport highway."

They heard sirens from somewhere north.

"Man, listen to that! Everything they've got is going out there. I wish we had a radio. Don't know what happened or how bad it is. Just said there was a plane crashed while landing."

"You think anyone was killed?"

"Hope not. I don't want to see that."

"Maybe we shouldn't go."

"You've got a point. Maybe we shouldn't. I just thought it was something you should see. You know how I am about fires. Every time the fire engine goes by, we follow it. We haven't missed a fire since you've been at the shop. Got to see everything that happens! I hate to miss anything. . . You decide. You don't want to go, we won't go."

The boy was silent for a long time. "Let's go."

"You've got to be curious in this life," Jack told him. "If you don't want to know everything that's going on, you never learn anything."

At Redwood Road the street was dark. Few lights and hardly any traffic. The sirens moaned louder. Across Redwood Road the street narrowed and entered pasture land and big open fields. A huge red glare came from the direction of the airport.

"It's burning, all right," Jack said. "A hell of a thing . . . never had an accident at this airport. None I can remember."

The narrow street made a sharp right turn to the north - the direction of the airport. At the airport highway a police car blocked the intersection. Flares burned on the street. Two officers with flashlights were directing traffic. An ambulance roared by, followed by three police cars and another ambulance. Then two wreckers and two fire engines.

"Man, everything in town is going out there." Jack shook his head in dismay. They parked near a service station.

"This is as far as we go. We'll have to walk. The only traffic they are letting through is emergency." Jack moved off quickly. "They sure didn't waste any time getting this highway closed off."

Jack and Andy joined a group walking west toward the airport. They were careful to stay as far away from the screaming emergency cars as possible. The red glow smoldered.

"It's on the runway," Jack said, now sounding despondent. "Not very far from the highway. Must have come down hard and fast to stop there."

An ambulance raced by coming from the crash site. Its siren screaming.

"Good God!" Jack exclaimed. "Look at that!"

In the back of the ambulance, it appeared that bodies were stacked like logs.

Andy couldn't believe it. He cried out, "Are they dead, Jack?"

"I don't know . . . hope to hell not . . . maybe just taking them to the hospital to get fixed up. I hope so." Jack knew better. "Come on, let's go. We can get down to the end of the runway."

They moved quickly with a crowd to a fence running adjacent to the runway. A line of police officers stopped them from going further. They wanted to get closer and see better but what they witnessed would follow them for the rest of their lives. Ambulance after ambulance streamed by, racing to the hospital. Each was filled with injured people stacked almost on top of each other. It was a shocking scene. Who could have known this would happen? Just minutes earlier, the passengers sailed in from the sky and looked down on the lights of the city below. They were looking forward to being in the city and seeing friends and family. Perhaps they were thinking of the fine meal they were going to have and how pleasant it would be. The airport flight path brought them over fields and houses, and straight ahead to the runway and the airport. It was the last thing many of the passengers ever saw.

In the darkness, Jack and Andy stumbled along a ditch to get a little closer. They could see a circle of fire engines around the red glow.

"We could get through the fence and over to the runway," Jack said.

"Let's stay here," Andy answered.

They could now make out the broken plane. Flames leaped into the sky and they made out a broken wing and the fire engines pumping and spraying.

More ambulances raced by going to the city as two more tow trucks headed into the airport.

"What do they do with the tow trucks?" Andy asked.

"Maybe they've got to try to tear it open to get inside."

After a while the glow began faded and then darkened. The fire had been extinguished. Three ambulance screamed by, but no more came from the city. The crowd started to dissipate, heading back to Redwood Road.

"Well, I guess we will read about it in the paper," Jack added. "We'd better get back."

"Do you think a lot of people were killed?"

"Those things hold about a hundred and twenty passengers." He looked over his shoulder and shook his head. "It's a hell of a thing to happen, Andy."

"I don't think I want to ride in one."

"I haven't been in a plane since I was in the army." Jack responded. "I made a few flights in Alaska. It was really rough flying up there. I'm not scared of them, they just make me sick, like being seasick. Maybe I wouldn't get sick in one of those jets. I don't know. I'm in no hurry to find out.

"It's just luck, Andy. You live a long time or you have bad luck and die quickly. I hope there weren't any kids on that plane. That's the worst thing - when kids get killed. It's different when older people get killed. You figure, well they've had quite a bit of life, but a kid hasn't had time to really learn or do things. It's sure a bad deal when a kid gets killed. I've seen so many and read about so many. It just seems like every year there's going to be a certain number of kids killed. They get hit by cars, they drown, they fall off cliffs, they ride their sled into a car, they fall off a horse, they fall out of a tree - the ice on the river breaks and they go through. My God, Andy, all the ways there are for a kid to die. You've sure got to have a lot of luck just to stay alive."

Jack gesticulated wildly and needed to talk.

"A cousin of mine in Idaho - it was a real shame. He was the nicest kid in the world. I visited him one summer and we went down to the Bear River and fished. Big carp there. Biggest damn carp I ever saw. Two and three feet long . . . catfish like monsters in that river. He showed me how to catch them. Damn, we had a good time that day catching those big fish. Had to wade out in the marsh to get to the edge of the river. Big river . . . widest river I've ever seen. . . and leeches in the marsh . . . I never saw leeches before. They get up your pant legs and start sucking your blood. My cousin showed me how to get them off . . . got to be real careful. We had to sit down and take the leeches off. We laughed and laughed.

"Everything we did that day was fun. He was one of the nicest people I've ever known, Andy. Kind and good and never hurt anybody. That fall, he was down at the river fishing alone and slipped and fell in and drowned. He was fourteen. Dammit, he was only fourteen!"

They reached the car and drove back to town. It was dark and quiet; only the lights from distant farm houses and the lights of the city to the east. The sirens were silent.

Breaking the silence, Andy said, "I saw a guy get killed. When I sold papers I went into a bar. It was full of men - this guy got shot."

" You saw that? Where?"

"Second South."

"Dangerous place," Jack interrupted.

"We always went into the bars to sell papers. They were loud. On this night, there were a few women in the back booths, maybe hookers, cuz I had seen them before at the hotels. I think some had kids at my school."

"Where?"

"I told your where."

"No, I mean what bar?"

"Club Loco, it's a rough bar," said Andy.

Club Loco was small and dark. It was on West Second South in the back of an empty lot and isolated from the rows of pool halls, beer joints and cheap hotels that lined both sides of the street.

The bar was owned by Rubio, a tough, ex-Army Ranger from Colorado. He had a reputation for bad things and his customers feared him. He always had an entourage around him, like a movie star. Andy's mom warned him, "Stay away from him, Andy." She said he was evil and would drug people and hurt them, hushing her voice as she spoke. "Please stay away," she warned.

"When I went in the bar it was real dark," Andy told Jack. "And, it was packed. Guys were standing at the bar, I was scared at first. I didn't want to see someone who knew my mom and would rat me off. I could barely make out anyone until my eyes adjusted. Rubio, the owner, was sitting at the end of the bar. He was dressed like a movie gunfighter, black clothes and wearing a gun in a holster. Do you know him, Jack?"

"No, not at all, I don't go to those places," answered Jack.

"Well, anyway, Rubio looks like a pit bull . . . real mean looking. The pool table in the back had a light hanging over the green top. It was like an island of light surrounded by the dark. I was walking toward the light when Rubio grabbed my arm. He told me to hurry and sell my papers and get out. He said the "chotas" would catch me in the bar and get him in trouble. After he let me go and I moved towards the pool table again."

"What's chotas?" Jack interrupted.

"Cops, Jack . . . Geez," Andy scolded, as though Jack should know Spanish slang. "Then there was this big EXPLOSION, so loud, my ears popped and were ringing. Then, it got real quiet and I smelled something burning-like and I saw the smoke from the gun . . . then everyone started yelling and swearing!

"Rubio yelled, 'Who shot him? Who shot him?'

"Over at the pool table, one guy said he shot him because, 'he was getting stupid.'

"Can you believe that, Jack?"

"No, of course not." Jack said narrowing his eyes. "But I know drinking makes people stupider."

"When I got closer to the pool table I could see blood pouring from the man's head. He was halfway on the pool table and the top of his head was gone."

"Oh for God's sake! Andy, don't talk about it. You'll have bad thoughts."

Andy was now going full steam ahead - gushing out his secret experience.

"There was blood all over, even on other people. Rubio swore at the guy who did the shooting. He got in his face. He yelled at him to get out and take the guy he shot with him. Rubio shouted that no one was leaving and told the bartender to lock the doors. I was so scared I couldn't move and I started crying. I didn't want to but I did. One of the ladies from the booths pulled me away towards the door. Her perfume was strong. She was so close, like bear hugging me. I almost threw up.

"They wrapped the guy in something and carried him out the back door to the alley. Rubio got madder 'cuz blood was spilling on the floor. He screamed he was going to kill them for making a mess and not wrapping the guy's head. He ordered some people to clean the floor and walls. He cut the green cloth from the pool table and peeled it off. It was soaked in blood. The bartender washed the pool table with soap and water.

"Rubio told me to quit crying, even though I already stopped. He said, 'You're not hurt. Quit crying! Go home and don't tell your mom you were here. Don't tell nobody! Don't talk to anyone about this or else.' He said the man wasn't lucky and that no one will miss him. Then, he unlocked the door, turned the music on loud again, and let me out. I ran all the way home.

"Just like you said Jack, no luck for that guy. He got killed, no luck I guess huh?"

"You've got luck, Andy," Jack said, amazed at the story. "You've got luck. I know it. You'll live a long time. A long, long time, Andy. Don't worry."

The story exhausted Jack. He felt guilty for taking the boy to the plane crash and for all the talk about people dying. This was a bad experience for the boy, he thought. Think about what you do to this boy before you run off like a chicken without a head, he scolded himself in silence.

The boy had lived a lifetime before he met Jack, which maybe explained his many moods - sometimes making it difficult for Jack to know how Andy would feel each day or even from hour to hour. Andy had a temper that flared occasionally, and sometimes his sullen moods needed to be countered with careful words. But, he also had possessed a warm almost smiling feeling. He made everyone a friend and showed a singing happiness that brightened the world.

Gosh, what a distance this boy has traveled in such a short time, thought Jack. From the streets and bars to the elite world of tennis clubs and tournament competition. Experiences a world apart. In terms of intensity and trauma, the journey was much greater than the drive from one side of town to another. You need to take it slow with the boy, he told himself. Be careful what you say, and especially what you do. Bring out the best in him, impact him with goodness. No more hairbrained ambulance chases or talk about death and violence. The boy deserves better. Be a good teacher and mentor. He deserves it.

Jack dropped the boy off without saying a word. Before Andy disappeared into his house, he turned and yelled, "Don't worry, Jack, we both have the luck, you'll see."

Jack drove away feeling empty, alone and stupid.

On a beautiful October evening while practicing at the park, a rising wind sent dried leaves scattering across the courts. The overhead lights on the red courts swayed gently, then jerked with some gusts. The sky darkened from the west and a flare of lightning told of what was to come.

"Let's get out of here," Andy said, as a great clap of thunder rocked them. "Geez, rain! Let's go!"

Just as they slammed the car doors, the storm hit and a fast rain splashed down. The wind roared through the giant cottonwoods, making the sound of a great river and the court lights danced and swung like frantic bells.

A high flash of white lightening turned everything electric and the rain seemed to pour out of barrels. The overhead lights now circled like windmills, and the large hot bulbs exploded in flares of fire and glass - whirling downward and scattering across the courts. One after another, they popped like fireworks.

Lightning controlled the sky and thunder shook the tall pines. The gutter and roadway filled quickly into a fast moving flood. The windshield wipers sloshed back and forth, and through the wet smear they sat and watched the magnificent light show and wild storm. It was like being alone in a mountain forest, caught in a cloudburst.

Within a few minutes, perhaps a half hour at most, all the lights were gone and the storm had blown itself out. The wind disappeared and it was quiet. Streaks of lightning and thunder came now from up in the eastern mountains. The rain had almost stopped as they drove slowly away from the courts. Every light in the park was extinguished.

That was the end of the night tennis season at the Liberty Park courts.

The first snow arrived without warning. Saturday was a fine warm fall day with crisp clear fresh air. But by early Sunday morning storm clouds from the north controlled the sky and swiftly filled all the valley. By nine-thirty, the snowfall began, small flakes at first, scattering in a gusty cold wind. Then, the wind calmed and the sky grew dark, gray and silent. The flakes came larger and thicker until it was impossible to see across the street. The heavy snow fell silently. Traffic slowed and the streets quieted. Tree boughs bent, weighed down with thick white snow and bushes and lawns transformed into a winter wonderland. The last remaining flowers were covered with the cold velvet whiteness.

The first snow in northern Utah seldom lasts long. A day or two later, it could be warm and sunny again with little evidence that winter had made a visit. But soon, the new season takes control and the temperature drops and one storm after another arrives. Winter.

For Andy and Jack, winter changed everything. Tennis was only a subject of discussion, it was back to work, school, and enduring the months of darkness and cold. For Jack, the problems he pushed into some corner or tossed into a drawer or hid in a file, came out to challenge him. They demanded his attention and he worried. The summer had passed so quickly. It wasn't likely winter would hurry. It never did.

"Man, I've sure got to get down to business," Jack said, shaking his head. "I'm way behind on my bills and I've got to get out there and find some more customers. If not, this whole place will go down the drain."

"Too much tennis, huh?" Andy asked, gingerly.

"Too much time. When we started I didn't know how much time the tennis would take. I'll have to get at it and use this winter to make up for lost time."

"I'll help," Andy offered.

"There's a lot you can do. Clean the place up. I suspect it will take you all winter. Do some deliveries. Yeah, there are lots of ways you can help."

"Maybe we ought to drop the tennis."

"Oh, no. Not now. I know you're going to make it, Andy. For me, it's like a guy whose never had a winning race horse and all of a sudden he finds maybe he's got one. He can't give up. He'll put every cent he's got into making that horse a winner. It's his big chance to do something great." He paused, then looked at Andy. "That's how I feel about you, Andy. Maybe you're another Pancho Gonzales. You just remember to tell them I got you started. Just don't forget that."

"I'll tell them, Jack. You bet, I'll tell them. You're

106

the best tennis coach ever."

"Okay," Jack laughed. "I know and you know. All you've got to do is prove it."

"Sure. Wait until next summer."

"Yeah, Andy," Jack said, pushing out his chest. "Just wait until next summer."

A few nights later, Jack worked a big job on the small press and Andy sat at the counter and studied. The talk turned to Jack's ex-wife - as it did occasionally.

"Was she pretty?" Andy asked.

"Yes. She was pretty."

"You liked her a lot, didn't you?"

"Yes."

"I don't see why she went away."

"She had reasons, I guess."

"Do you still like her?"

Jack stopped and looked at his feet. Shaking his head, he answered slowly, "No. Not any more. It took a long time. But not any more."

Andy knew Jack was sad, "I'm sorry."

Damn it, Jack thought to himself. Twelve-years-old and the kid knows more about me than anyone in the whole damn world.

"I don't think I ever want to get married," Andy started.

"It isn't the marrying. It's just liking someone so much. You like them so much it hurts. It hurts all the time."

"I don't like that."

"Maybe it won't happen. Maybe you'll be lucky. Yes, you'll be lucky. It won't hurt like that for you."

"Sometimes," Andy said, but paused, "sometimes, I think I don't want to grow up."

"Neither do I."

"But you are grown up."

"Yeah, but a lot of days it's not much fun."

"I'd like to stay twelve forever."

"Just remember the good days you've had," Jack advised him. "The good days go by and you don't realize how fast they're going by, and then you look back and say I sure had a swell time, back then." His gaze seemed somewhere else, focusing on some long lost vision. "I sure had a swell time. It was real great . . . And, I didn't know at the time how great it was. You look back, Andy, and wish you had known what a good time you were having."

Saturday afternoon while Jack worked the press, and Andy and his friend, Manuel, sat at the table eating cookies and laughing, the building owner, Bill Roberts, stopped by.

He stopped at the counter, looked around, shook his head. "By God, Jack, if you don't get this place cleaned up better, you'll have the fire department on me, sure."

"Yeah," Jack answered, not missing a beat. "I guess you're right, Bill. We'll get at it."

"You said that last time I was down here. Last month. You've been saying that, honestly, since last year. It don't look one bit better."

"We'll get at it this week end. Sure."

The landlord glared at Andy and Manuel. "Anyhow, I didn't come down here for that . . . It's about these two. You know what they've been doing?"

"Well, you mean today? Right now?"

"I mean half an hour ago. They were up on the fifth floor dropping water balloons out the window, down onto the alley where people walk." He was getting hot, "Now I've told you about that before, Jack. I've told you about that before, all right."

Jack wiped the sweat from his forehead, "I didn't know they . . . "

"And, a damn good many other foolishness those kids been doing," Bill added. "Having them down here is your business as long as you pay the rent. By the way, Jack, could you possibly get caught up with your rent? If possible? Give us a whole lot of printing and put it on the rent. I'd appreciate it."

"Why, yes. I'll . . . "

"Now I don't want to hear any more about water balloons being dropped or running through the halls upstairs or making a lot of noise or a half a dozen other things." He looked at the boys. "I get complaints about these kids . . . Jack, no hard feelings but I got other people in this building."

"Bill, you're absolutely right. I'll see . . . "

Bill interrupted again, "Just keep those kids down here, will you? And, see about your rent Jack, will you? I don't worry, but it upsets my bookkeeper. She gets upset and nags me all day. I'd appreciate it, Jack. Just get us a whole lot of printing and put it on the rent."

"You bet, Bill. We'll clean this place up and I'll get some of your jobs finished and . . . "

"Thanks, Jack. Nice to talk to you. Good night."

"Night, Bill."

When the door closed, Jack gave Andy and Manuel

a stern look. Andy watched him carefully, not knowing whether to leave or stay.

"You guys trying to get me in trouble? Dropping water balloons after all the times I've told you! You want us to get thrown out of the building? We get pushed out of here and that finishes it. I can't move anywhere else. Don't have the money to move. I'm hanging in here like a fly in a spider-web. You want to lose this place?"

"No, Jack," Andy answered, sincerely.

"We won't do it any more," Manuel added.

"You said that last time."

"When was last time?" Andy asked, now mischievous.

"I don't remember. But it wasn't very damn long ago, I'll bet. No more going upstairs unless you're with me, understand? You come and go through the alley."

"What if it's snowing bad?"

"All right, use the front door, but go quietly and don't go through the front hall while the janitor's cleaning up. You know it makes him wild when you track through his mopping."

Andy laughed, "Yeah, he gets real mad."

"Don't laugh. It isn't funny. I don't want any more foolishness. Get the picture?"

"Yeah, Jack, we get the picture."

"So, this weekend you can help me clean up this mess?"

"We cleaned up last month," Andy protested. "We took out boxes and boxes of stuff."

"Somehow, it doesn't look any different than last year."

"Was the fire department here?"

"Oh, they look in once in a while. They don't like it, but they don't say much. They look around and make some grunts and groans and do a lot of pointing. How can I run a print shop without a lot of paper around?"

"Sure takes a lot of paper, doesn't it, Jack?"

"Lots and lots of paper."

To the left of the alley door was a large room that had been a photo lab for a drug store chain. It was closed when they moved to a larger building. Now the room was for storage of odds and ends. Jack had an idea that part of the room could be converted into a backboard for practicing tennis by moving some old furniture and mattresses.

One weekend Jack, Andy and two of his friends, Manuel and Jimmy, (promised tickets to a movie and candy money) moved everything away from the back wall and into some smaller rooms, wherever there was space.

"How about Mr. Roberts? Maybe he won't like this," Andy asked.

"Whew! That stuff gets heavy," Jack replied. "He won't care. He'll think we've done him a favor clearing this space . . . Now he's got room to move things around."

"I'll bet he finds something to put here sooner or later."

"That's possible. That guy never throws anything away. Every hotel he's had, there's stuff here he'll never sell or use. That dentist's chair for example. It's so old it's an antique. I saw one like that in a western picture."

"How'd he get the chair?"

"Oh, he keeps stuff when people can't pay the rent.

This dentist probably couldn't pay, or maybe he just moved out and left the chair. Roberts grabs what's left for rent money. If the guy wants it back, he's going to have to pay up all the rent he owes."

"You said it," Andy commented, looking around. "Roberts never throws anything."

"Well, Andy, we move these mattresses and that ought to give you enough room. Paint a line across the wall and you're in business, an indoor backboard."

"The ceiling's too low and the steam pipes are in the way."

"You want the moon, too?"

"No. I just need a place to practice."

"We'll move these mattresses and you paint a stripe on that wall and you've got it. It's better than nothing."

"Well . . . I guess so. Yeah, it's all right."

Andy practiced after school. The low ceiling was a real obstacle, but he could practice forehand and backhand strokes if he didn't hit the ball too hard and flat without much topspin. It was better than nothing, especially since the courts at Liberty Park were under two feet of snow.

Around seven o'clock, Andy and Jack would leave to eat. If the weather was bad or Jack was low on funds, they ate in the shop. There was a stock of canned gods, pork and beans, chili, sardines, macaroni, spaghetti, beef stew, usually a box of crackers and always cookies. There was an electric hot plate to cook and Jack taught Andy about preparing a meal.

"I'll show you how to do hobo cooking - like the hobo's do." Jack got everything ready. "Okay, like this.

Open the can, but don't cut the lid off. Leave a piece for a hinge. See, bend the lid back for the handle, and put the can on the stove. You've got to stir it, so it won't burn on the bottom. Get a rag to hold on to the lid so you won't burn your fingers."

"Like this?" Andy tried.

"That's it. Stir it up every few seconds. I'll get the paper plates and some forks, if we've got any left. And, find some napkins. Here, take this and get some drinks from the machine upstairs." He handed Andy some change. "Do you know how to make depression soup?"

"Depression soup? What's that?"

"During the big depression in 1931 things were real tough. No work and no money. So, you had to eat the best way you could. Rabbits, dandelions, make your own candy out of honey, buy stale cake. Man, you had to keep thinking how you were going to eat tomorrow. There was this one café you could get a bowl of hot water for a nickel. Then, you put ketchup in the hot water and you had depression soup."

"Ah, come on, Jack. That sounds terrible."

"You've learned something today. Got it? Every day learn something new. You can tell your mother you know how to hobo cook and how to make depression soup. So, when the next big depression comes along, you guys are all set. Every day you should learn something."

After dinner, Andy did his homework. Sometimes, Jack helped when he understood what it was about. Jack was number one in English composition and spelling, but math was another matter. He could figure out how many pieces of paper 4 x 6 inches could be cut out of a sheet of 19 x 24 inches and how many lines of pica type copy should go into 12 ems of 10 point type. But, the new math was something from outer space.

The work Andy did in the shop, besides sweeping up and throwing out, was regular print shop work. Gathering paper into sets. A set includes the original, duplicate and triplicate, each were printed separately, and usually on a different color of paper. They had to be hand gathered in proper order. Jack sat the stacks of paper on the table and Andy would take the triplicate, the duplicate, and then the original on top of the set. Nothing difficult about it, but it was important to keep focused so the colors weren't in the wrong order. Andy was very good at this, but it was monotonous work and when it was a large job he got tired and complained.

"Somebody's got to do it," Jack answered. "Can't get paid until the job's gathered and delivered. I've got the press to run. It's a big help when you do it. Besides, you're faster than I am."

When not running the press, Jack often recalled his army life during World War Two. There was no specific thing that triggered these memories - could be a song on the radio, something in the newspaper, someone he knew who was about to be drafted - but it would set Jack going and he thoroughly enjoyed talking about what was not, he made clear, the good old days, but often sounded like they were almost the good old days.

When Andy's friends or brother, James were there, he would laugh and say, "Here we go again. Fort Ord!"

Andy really didn't mind listening. It came straight from the horse's mouth, Jack had been there. It was not some imaginary play story on television.

"I'll tell you guys. In the army some weird things happen. Especially in that outfit I was with. Horse-drawn field artillery. We rode horses. It sounds unbelievable now even to me. I don't think the Pentagon even knew we existed. On paper, we were supposed to be a truck-drawn outfit. But those knot-heads in the Pentagon didn't know what was going on anywhere. They didn't even know Pearl Harbor would happen. We were guarding that whole part of the west coast with those old French Seventy-Fives made in France, maybe for Napoleon. Wood wheels.

"Every other week we would have to take the wheels off and put them in a creek to let them soak-up water so the wood wouldn't dry out and shrink. The iron rims might come loose. When we hit out on maneuvers, it was like covered wagon days. No, it was more like a circus. The Seventy-Fifth Field Artillery Battalion. I was in Battery A. A real swell bunch of guys. That was the only good part of the Army. Having a bunch of great guys like that. And tough! Man, that outfit made you tough. Up early in the morning. Fix your bunk. Get your saddle bags ready. Grab something to eat. Be ready when it was time to go - or else! Then out to the stable. Harness up your team. I was riding the lead pair at the time. There were three pair to a cannon or a caisson. The caisson carried the ammunition. You rode the left horse - lead, swing, wheel. The wheel pair were big with giant hooves to hold the gun back going downhill. Harness up your pair and watch you don't get kicked or stepped on.

"Oh, it was real fun early in the morning before the sun came up. Then, out to the gun park and hook-up. The pair I had were flighty and spooky, especially the off horse. You rode the near horse and had reins for the off horse. His name was Dean. Soon as we were hooked up, Dean was ready to go. Reared up in the air. Sometimes, I thought he'd fall over backwards on me. I'd lean over and talk soft to him - trying to calm him down. He'd snort and paw the dirt and jump up like a crazy fool. Horses don't have much sense. If it was windy and some paper blew across the gun park, some dumb horse would get spooked and take off. Man, I've seen mad runaways in the gun park. Take the bit in their teeth and go. Just take off, any direction, anything in their way just got trampled. Guys would fall off or get kicked and sometimes run over. Never anything serious, though. We were a lucky outfit. Never had anybody hurt bad. It was a good outfit. Lucky. Lots of loyalty and working together. I was sure proud of that outfit and all those guys. We sure had some good times together."

"I thought you hated the Army, Jack."

"Yeah, most of the time. The Army is something else. These guys weren't the Army. They were draftees, like me. Sure, there were some regular Army guys. It was a regular Army outfit. But the regular Army guys were being sent out on cadres to start new outfits, so after a few months it was mostly draftees. It was the draftees that won the war, believe me. Those regular Army guys didn't care how long it lasted. They were in for thirty years anyhow, and with all the build-up for the war and all the new outfits being formed, they had a better chance to get good ratings. Before the war in the regular Army, a guy would wait maybe ten years before he could make sergeant. Oh, they thought that Army life was a big deal. Board and room and clothes and a dollar a day to spend. Real crazy life."

Jack paused for a moment, then remembered another story. "We went on maneuvers one time to Hearst Ranch. That's a big place about ninety miles south of Fort Ord. Man, I'll say that was a big place. We never did see all of it. Maybe twenty-thousand troops down there in that maneuver. They sent us out a week ahead. Ninety miles. Took us three days to get there. Rest of them came down in trucks in three hours - took us three days. We left Fort Ord at sunrise and took a highway south. I'll tell you, if that wasn't a sight. We were strung out for miles. Each Battery separated a ways so traffic could get around us. Those horses clopping down the road made a noise like no one had ever heard. People came rushing out of their houses. I guess some of them thought they were being invaded. They had never seen anything like it. First, the guidon bearer and the First Sergeant and the Battery Commander and the other officers alongside to keep things closed up in order. Then the cannon and caisson of each gun section. Four sections. Then the headquarters section and supply sections and stable crew, all these with canvas-topped wagons to carry equipment. They were three batteries and headquarters battery to a battalion. And there were three battalions, the Seventy-Fourth, Seventy-Fifth , and Seventy-Sixth. What a show."

"Jack, it's nine o'clock. Time to go home."

"Okay. Get your things gathered up." Jack's revere was finished. "I hope that car starts without any trouble. It's cold as the dickens out there."

"I hope so, too. It's sure nice and warm in here."

"Yeah. These cold nights I almost hate to leave. Well, let's go."

"Can we stop and get a hamburger?"

"Sure."

"At the Arctic Circle. They've got the best hamburgers."

"All right."

Hitting a ball against a wall in a basement with low ceilings can get monotonous. It's the opponent who makes the game. The competition. The winning. Andy hit the ball against a wall hour after hour on cold winter days, as the steam pipes cracked and the snow piled up higher and higher against the frozen windows. Winter seemed to last forever.

Finally, a warm sunny spell partially melted the snow.

"Let's go to the park," Andy said. "Maybe the snow's melted on the courts. Maybe one is dry. I bet the one by Brian's shack is dry."

"I doubt it," Jack said. "The snow melts, but the courts are still wet."

"Let's go see. Maybe we could hit a few."

"Use the old balls then."

"All right. Can we?"

"We'll try it. Maybe we'll have an early spring."

"In California, they play all winter - outside."

"Yeah, they do."

"Bet that's great, being able to play all winter. If I had played all winter, I'd be pretty good now, huh?"

"You bet you'd be good. Here, we have to do the best we can. Let's take a broom so we can sweep the court if it's wet. Maybe we can get it fairly dry."

They parked near Brian's shop. Most of the windows were broken, but the door was securely shut. The two Coke machines stood side by side, one was unplugged. The other hummed faintly. Snow still stood in the shadowed places of the park, on the north side of trees and behind high bushes and below the shrubs. In corners of some of the courts were remnants of snow, melting where the sun touched it, the water making the narrow streaks. Andy got the broom and swept the wet spots on Court One.

"This is the driest. It always dries off first."

"Want a Coke?"

"Sure."

"If the machine works." Jack dropped in a dime and a nickel. He wasn't going to trust it with a quarter. A clanking noise replied and then a bottle came down, clunk. Another dime and nickel. He opened one bottle and the Coke was really cold for a change.

Andy had most of the wet spots swept over. "How is it, Jack?"

"Here's your Coke. Looks good. Won't hurt the old balls. Won't hurt nylon strings."

"Do I get a real good racquet this summer?"

"What kind?"

"Brian's got a Kramer Autograph I can have for fifteen."

"Stringed?"

"No. He said he'd do it now before summer and put in gut strings for only ten dollars."

"Twenty-five bucks."

"That's a lot of money, isn't it, Jack?"

"You know it."

"He's got cheaper ones with nylon strings."

"You've got a cheap racquet."

"I'll work real hard for a good racquet. That Kramer is the best. I could sure play good with a Kramer with gut strings."

"Well, let's see how good you practice today. Let's find out if banging the ball around in the basement has helped any."

Okay, I'll show you. I'm hitting harder, a lot harder."

"Get the racquets and balls. Show me how good you are."

The sun was still far to the southwest, but it looked warmer. It was nice to think about spring and summer being on the way. In the open spaces where the snow melted first, the grass was beginning to brighten. The ducks in the pond by the horseshoe pits were quacking and making a fuss.

Except for the pines, the trees were leafless and it was too early for buds. Several good warm days would bring them out and then everything would start again. In the long greenhouses, plants and flowers were ready to be placed out along the sidewalks and roads, and in the fancy-shaped flower beds that gardener's loved. On the other side of the tennis courts cement backboard, the swimming pool was partly filled with debris, leaves, broken limbs, paper, the leavings of the winter. Beyond the picnic ground, through the trees Andy could see the skeleton of the red Ferris wheel. It stood unmoving, waiting for the summer and the endless days filled with kids and laughter. Nearby, at the pagoda-shaped carousel building everything seemed lost and lonely; inside the horses were standing ready for the riders, waiting for the music to begin again and the rainbow lights to be switched on. Tossing their manes, they would gallop around the circle, announcing that the warm weather had arrived and that all of the park would soon be alive again.

Spring came with hesitation. More snow, sunny days that could be counted on fingers, some rain, a series of windstorms. School was a priority for Andy and tennis practice, when the courts were dry. And, there was work in the shop.

Jack set the three stacks of paper on the table, in proper order to be gathered into sets. He pushed a chair directly in front, got the glycerin bottle and poured a bit on the glycerin rag. This made the fingers sticky and paper easier to handle.

"Okay, you're all set. Gather all of it tonight. I want to deliver it tomorrow. You need ten dollars for the school trip to Rancho Lanes, so this job will get you the ten dollars. Otherwise, I don't have ten dollars to give you."

"What do I do?"

"It's triplicate. You've done it before. The white, canary and pink. Like this, pick up the pink first, then the canary on top, and the white on top of that. Simple. Even I can do it. Just don't get them missed up. Got it?"

"Yeah. I guess so."

"Some day you'll be the world's champion gatherer."

"I don't want to be the world's champion gatherer."

"Well. Somebody has to. Right now, for ten dollars to go to Rancho Lanes, you're it."

"All right. I'm it." Andy picked up a pink, a canary, a white.

"Do it right. Watch what you're doing. It has to be right. And hurry - so you'll get done before time to go home.

I'll pad it in the morning, delivered it, and get a check, I hope."

Jack went to the platen press where he fed envelopes for an hour. It was nearly nine o'clock.

"You through, Andy?"

"Just about." There was a stack in front of him.

Jack shut off the motor, stopping the press by using his left hand on the flywheel. He looked at the gathered sheets.

"What are you doing?" He leafed through the stack. "You've got the canary on top."

"I did it the way you told me."

"How could it be the way I told you? The white is always on top! It's always on top! Forever and ever the white copy is always on the top. Haven't you been told enough times? How could you come out with the canary on top?"

"I don't know. I just did it the way I thought you wanted it."

"Good God. It's so simple. It doesn't take any brains at all. The whole thing has got to be taken apart and gathered over." Jack dropped his shoulders and stood in one place. "Well, hell! There's no time for that now. You've got to get on the bus for home. Get your jacket and your books."

"Don't be mad," Andy pleaded. "I'm sorry. I'll stay and do it over."

"You can't stay and do it over. You have to catch the bus since we've got no car running tonight. You have to leave now and catch the bus."

"You don't have to get so mad."

"It's such a simple thing. Always the white on top.

You've gathered stuff before. How could you do it without the white on top? What's the matter, didn't you bring your brain today?"

"I forgot. I didn't mean to."

"Come on, let's go. There's no time to do anything about it now. I'll have to tear it apart and fix it in the morning. I won't be able to get it delivered early enough to get a check tomorrow. You'll just have to forget about going to Rancho Lanes."

"Everybody in my class is going."

"You didn't do the job right. I can't deliver it. I don't get paid, so you don't get ten dollars. Come on. Hurry. You have to catch the bus."

Jack was getting more and more angry. It burned into him. It was unreasonable, but there it was. All the way to the bus stop, he complained about how stupid it was. "If you can't do the job right, I'll get someone else! I'll have to get someone else." It was a lie and he knew it. But the boy took it seriously.

The bus came and Andy got on. As it pulled away from the curb he was at the back window looking tearfully out at Jack standing there on the walk. Jack was not looking at him, he stared blankly down the street.

The bus disappeared and Jack walked the half block to the alley and into the shop. The shop was empty when the boy was not there. When Andy was there, the placed seemed to glow with warmth.

He looked at the table with the misgathered forms. "Damn!"

He had envelopes to finish. Re-gathering the forms would have to wait until morning. He was too tired to do it now, too damn tired of a lot of things.

In the morning, the shop was dreary. Sometimes, on a morning like this, he didn't know why he kept up with it. He had to do something. He had to figure out some way to better his life - and his finances. With money to pay up all the bills everything would be great. He sat down to work on the forms and the boy appeared.

"Well, what are you doing here?"

The boy looked at him carefully, trying to judge his temper. "I couldn't sleep. I had to get here to do the job over."

"Where have you been?"

"I was in the rug room waiting for you."

"You're supposed to be in school. You'll catch it for not going to school."

"I don't care. You were mad. I couldn't sleep, anyhow. I have to get those gathered right."

Jack stared at the boy and then looked at the forms. His eyes scanned the shop as the big steam pipes cracked. He remembered the first day the boy had come down to the shop, carrying the big bag of evening papers, his hands almost frozen from standing on the corner in the bitter cold.

"You'd better get to school, Andy. You'll get in trouble if you miss. I'll take care of this. I'll re-gather it and I'll take care of it. You can't miss school just for this."

"You were mad and I couldn't sleep and I got up early and walked uptown. I waited for you in the rug room so I could fix the job so it would be right."

"It's all right. I didn't mean to get so mad. It's just you needed the ten dollars to go bowling and I had to get the job delivered and paid for so you'd have the ten dollars. I didn't care about the job. You needed the money and the only way I could get it right now was to get the job delivered and pick up the check. Come on, let's go get the bus and you go to school. I'll write an excuse for you saying you were sick and had to be late. You'd better go to school. It's important."

"You're not mad at me?"

"No, of course not. I just lost my temper because I wanted to get that money for you,"

"You won't get someone else?"

"Andy! Hell no. Come on, let's get you back to school." Jack took a long look at the boy. Damn, he thought, why does he care what I say or do? Why does he care at all? Why am I so stupid? I don't know . . . don't know . . . don't know.

Then came a succession of warm days in May and all the boys of Andy's age returned to the park courts for regular play. He hadn't seen some since October and there were striking physical changes. When boys reach thirteen or fourteen they get taller, heavier, and take on a more grown-up look. They are reluctant to leave childhood and the toy-playing stage, yet eager to grow up and enter the adult world - and all its mysterious freedoms. Some of the thirteen-year-olds were several inches taller, and two of the fourteen-year-olds were as tall as Jack. Andy had gained about half an inch and four pounds.

"I hope I'm taller next year," Andy remarked. "If I was taller I could serve a lot better. You think I'll be real tall, Jack?"

"Any real tall people in your family?"

"Not my mother. And my dad - haven't seen him since I was a little kid. Three-years-old. He wasn't any taller than you. I don't think he was."

"How about your uncles? Grandfather?"

"Don't know them. My mom hates my Dad's side, so I don't know much. My grandfather's tall though."

"How tall? Six feet?"

"He works a farm in New Mexico. He's almost seventy-years-old, I guess, and he still works his farm. I think he's maybe six feet."

"You've got a chance then. I'll tell you, Andy, all the exercise you're getting and the good food and vitamins, I don't see any reason you shouldn't be six feet tall."

"I'd like to be as tall as Pancho. Maybe I could serve as hard as Pancho then."

"It helps playing if you're tall. You can get a better serve and cover the net better - lot's of advantages. But, there has been plenty of small players who were great. Anyhow, you do the best you can and next year or the next you'll grow up and have a good long reach. If you play good now, you'll play better then. Being tall isn't so important. You can beat a lot of tall men now. You just know the game better than they do. Timing, coordination and being quick on your feet - and lots of practice. That's what counts."

Saturday at two o'clock they drove to the park.

"You're sure he'll be there?"

"I shouldn't be leaving this early," Jack said, more to himself than Andy. "I've got jobs to run off."

"You can come back. I want to get it now. Brian said it would be ready at two."

The door to Brian's shack was open. Three of the

courts were being used; two girls, one tall and the other short were batting a ball back and forth on court One. They squealed in ecstasy every time the ball went over the net.

"Hi, Brian," Andy announced.

"Hi, Andy. Hi, Jack."

"Got it ready?"

"Strung it this morning." Brian took a racquet off the wooden pegs on the wall and handed it to Andy.

The boy took the racquet gently in both hands, as if he was receiving the Holy Grail. He held it out and looked at it, turning it around and running his hands over it.

"Isn't it neat, Jack? Isn't it?"

"Terrific."

A small color photo of Jack Kramer sat on the wide throat and below his inscription, "Jack Kramer Autograph."

Andy held it out and his eyes went dreamy. With this racquet, he thought, everyone at the club better look out! He was ready now. The warrior was at last armed with the ultimate weapon. The matador holding the invincible sword. No one could stop him now.

"It's beautiful, Jack. Hit some with me. I want to try it out."

"I've got to get back," he start, but then agreed. "All right. Get my racquet and some balls out of the car."

"Buy some new balls, Jack. I need new ones with this racquet."

"Oh, all right. Go get my racquet."

Jack took out his wallet. "Twenty-five?"

"Plus sales tax," Brian paused, "Oh, forget the tax. Make it twenty-five, even."

Jack took out ten ones, a five, and a folded-up, dirty

slip of green paper. "This check is good. One of my customers. I've been saving it." He signed the check and handed it to Brian.

"A can of balls, too." Jack said, "Two, twenty-five, aren't they?"

"Forget it. I'll throw in a can of balls."

"Thanks, Brian."

"He's a good kid. I like helping him out."

"Do you think he'll make it?" Jack asked. "I mean, I know he's got ability. Does a kid outside of the club really have a chance?"

"I'll tell you, Jack, every kid that's ranked for the city, the state and the Intermountain area is from the club. Nobody here at the park is ranked. But, he's better than any kid I've ever seen play here."

"But nobody from the park has ever been in the rankings?"

"Sure haven't."

Andy returned with Jack's racquet. "Let's go! I want to try out my new racquet."

"Here's a can of balls. Now you're all set."

"With this racquet I can beat everybody. You'll see, Jack. Now, I can really play."

"Practice some serves for a few minutes. I want to talk to Brian."

"Okay. Hurry!" Andy ran to the first vacant court.

"At the fall tournament at the club, Trane said for me to bring Andy up to the club. He was asking about Andy and who he was and who I was. Does that really mean anything?"

"Maybe it means Andy can get a membership,"

Brian said, thoughtfully.

"They're going to give it to him?"

"Trane wouldn't give away wooden nickels. If Andy's got the money, he can join."

"Man, now that's real generous of him."

"Well, in a way. They're pretty restrictive up there. If Trane didn't approve, he couldn't get a membership - even if he had twice the money."

"I had the idea he might help Andy with lessons and let him practice there - once in awhile - so he could get some good competition."

"You can ask."

"I haven't got the hundred dollars to buy a membership. If I had it, I'd get it right now. I've got lots of money problems."

"Call him up."

"I don't know. I'd sure feel like an idiot if he just meant that Andy could get in the club if he could buy a membership. I'd have to tell him I couldn't afford it. I suppose to him, a hundred dollars is small change."

"He makes out all right."

"Ah, Brian. Tennis is no sport for poor relations."

"Andy's getting along fine. He wouldn't be doing much better at the club."

"Probably not. But what happens if I leave town? I've got a bug about maybe going to Los Angeles. Lots of good jobs down there with security. I sure don't have any security here. If I leave, it won't be this year, maybe not next year, I don't know. But after that, if I leave who is going to keep Andy interested in tennis? There's no one to get him up to the club but me. He lives ten miles on the other side of town. I'll have to work something out."

"He should live on the east side and have parents with money. Then, he wouldn't have any problems."

"Brilliant observation."

"One things for sure. If Andy hadn't had his troubles, and you hadn't had yours, you would have never met the boy."

"Just dumb luck, I guess," Jack smiled.

There were days Andy played badly. Jack tried to figure out a rhythm for these bad days. Should Andy practice hard the day before a tournament, take it easy, or not practice at all? He was not an early morning player. He could easily lose a morning match and then play tough in the late afternoon. Jack planned that Andy would get to bed very early the night before a morning match. It seemed to make a difference in how he played. Either he played well or he didn't. It was simply that Andy was an afternoon player. Fortunately, as he grew older, most of his matches would be in the afternoon or evening.

Jack was strict about Andy getting enough sleep. Andy told him every day what he had eaten. His evening meal was chosen to balance out the day with a salad or eggs or fish or meat. Jack had him drink ten ounces of orange or grapefruit juice every day. There was a large bottle of vitamins at the shop and Andy got one most days - and two during tournaments. Jack kept salt tablets in the car for the heat, and Amitone for any sudden stomach upsets.

Jack watched over Andy's health as carefully as a horse trainer looks out for an expensive thoroughbred.

Practice was any hour available, sometimes early

morning. It was a painful time for Jack. The only way to help Andy's morning play was to make him get on the courts before seven. They were both only half awake but it was especially nice in the park that time of day. Cool and with a morning mist. Without people or cars it was quiet, and birds and squirrels were busy on the wide lawns. From the nearby aviary, tropical birds made the strange songs and cries of their jungle and island homelands. Fountains of water from sprinklers sprayed silvery in the sun.

There were few other players on the courts at this time. Some got in a set or two before work. Others, who had more time, practiced intently for coming tournaments.

Jack set up a training schedule. "I want you to hit everything to his backhand. Everything. You've got to work hard on this. You've been putting easy shots to the forehand and down the center, just where the other guy wants it."

"It's hard to hit to the backhand all the time."

"Of course it's hard. If it was easy you wouldn't have any problems."

Again and again, he worried about the time Andy needed to make up skills he didn't have. The little knowledge of tennis he had, he tried to give quickly to Andy. He read books. And, Andy watched all the good players and, when possible, played them. Andy was getting some good training and a great deal of bad.

"You'll have to do the best you can," Jack told him. "You've got to learn in one year what should take three. You've got to find the best way to swing and serve. You've got to be thinking and learning all the time. Every day the courts are dry, you've got to be out there working."

"I'll beat this game," Andy told him. "I'm going to

be champ. I'm going up to the tennis club and murder those kids."

The summer afternoon boiled with heat. The hard courts caught and held the heat, reflecting it like a blast furnace. Jack came back to the park at lunch time, often eating at The Jade.

"I played Mr. Carter," Andy old him. "Almost beat him. I had him running back and forth. Boy, he really had to go. I was eight-six, six-four. He wants to play again tomorrow morning."

"You mean we've got to get up early again tomorrow?"

"You want me to get good practice in the mornings, don't you?"

Jack sighed, "I'll pick you up same time as today."

When the evening cooled, they returned to the park.

On stormy days, play was erratic. Andy would lose his temper. "I can't hit the ball right when the wind blows."

"You'll have to learn. They won't stop a match for the wind. The one who plays best in the wind, takes it."

Andy hated the wind. It blew his serve out and he misjudged the ball curving to him.

"I hate this game!" he said, after a bad return into the net. "Can't play in the wind! This is a stupid game."

"You're right."

"What are we doing out here in this wind then? It's going to rain, anyhow."

"When it rains, we'll stop. Get this." Jack hit a forehand.

Grumbling, Andy returned it. A gust of wind caught the ball, carried it out.

"Oh, great!" he screamed. He made a gesture, as if to throw his racquet into the net.

"Don't you throw that new racquet!" Jack shot up to the net. "Now listen here, hothead. I don't like this wind any better than you. It's getting cold and I'm tired and I've got a million things I should be doing at the shop. You just get with it and play like you mean it. You aren't out here to have fun. You're out here to learn how to play in the wind. If I can stand it, so can you. Get the picture?"

Andy's face contorted, and he grumbled. Back at the baseline, he waited for the ball. He looked across at Jack and smiled. "Okay, Jack, okay. You're the coach, Jack. You say it, I do it."

"That's the idea," Jack said, smiling back at him.

The second summer for Andy was a giant step. From raw novice he was now more confident, more aggressive. He understood the workings of the tournaments. He knew or played against most of the seeded players. He was familiar with the courts where the tournaments were held. He knew the officials of the tennis associations. He now had quite a wide acquaintance of players, young and old.

He was drawn to the older players - the college players and men just a few years out of college. These, he wanted to play and beat. Some were more than willing to practice with him and help him. When he improved and played well, it made them feel good, having been a part in his improvement. It was as if it also gave them a sense of improvement.

There were others who would have nothing to do with him. Some who just did not like to bother with kids, and others who were afraid that in time the boy might beat them. This would mean a loss of face. They would not chance it.

One of the regulars at the park was Doug Wixom. He lived in Salt Lake City but was a junior at BYU, thirty-five-miles south. He worked a part-time office job mornings, and played tennis at the park courts afternoons and evenings. Wixom was a tough player. He took up tennis seriously in high school, very late to think about being a top player. Practice and a stubborn determination helped him to improve dramatically. He hoped to obtain a tennis scholar-ship at his school. If he could improve enough to impress the coach, he might have a chance. He badly needed the schol-arship to finish school.

Wixom was not well-liked by the upper-class at the tennis club. He had a wild temper, talked angrily to himself when playing badly and was inclined to throw his racquet after a miserable shot. After breaking two good racquets, he kept an old one handy for throwing - it took a terrific beat-ing. Andy was afraid of Doug at first but watched him play at every chance.

"I'd like to practice with him," Andy admitted to Jack.

"Well, go ask."

"I'm afraid. I don't think he likes kids. He hits the ball real hard."

"He throws a racquet real hard, too. You make a dumb play, he'd likely throw it at you."

Andy laughed. "I'd sure learn to get out of the way."

"When he isn't playing with someone, why don't you ask if you can work out with him?"

"You ask him."

"I don't think he'd like that. You ever see him play a kid?"

"No."

"Maybe he's seen you play. If he has he'll know you're a hard hitter, and you run."

"He's been here some afternoons. He's got a jump-rope and he gets over there on the grass and jumps rope. Then he runs around the park. One day, he ran around five times. How far is it around the park?"

"Just a guess, about a mile. Maybe a little more."

"Five miles! That's a long run. He does push-ups, too."

"You didn't think much of jumping rope when Mrs. Sherry told you Patty did."

"Ah, that's different. Boxers jump rope, too."

"I guess you need a jump rope now."

"I don't know, I'll think about it."

Wixom was playing a match with another college student. Andy watched. When he made a good play, Wixom smiled like he owned the court. When he made a bad play, he raised his racquet and cursed the skies - and all the tennis gods who weren't for him. He was tall, but not slender, and he had a mop of red hair and a homely face. It made quick changes from smiling good-naturedly to a scornful, steaming wrath. He had a big windup serve. Andy watched his serve and thought about it. It wasn't the way Jack had taught him, or the type of serve Jack admired. But, it was effective. He didn't make many double faults.

After a set, the college student left and went to his car. Doug practiced serving and Andy studied him. He wanted to hit the ball that hard, and serve it so fast the other guy couldn't see it. The only way he was ever going to get that good was playing with guys like Doug. The other boys at the park just didn't have the ability.

Doug was gathering up the balls.

"Want to hit some?"

Doug stopped and gave Andy a quizzical look. The skinny kid didn't seem to be a day over ten. His racquet was almost twice his size.

"You hit the ball hard?" he asked.

"Sure."

"You a tough player, kid?"

"I'm tough."

"I can't waste time practicing with kids who just bat the ball. I hit it hard and you better hit it hard back. You get in the way and the ball hits you and you cry, you can go right home to mama." He waited for Andy to respond but Andy just stared at him. "Okay kid, get over there and let's see if you're tough."

"I'm tough," Andy said.

He got ready, holding his racquet tightly, standing ready, his feet braced a foot apart, crouching down a bit, ready to move quickly.

The ball came at him. Not too fast but low. He stepped into it, swung hard, hit it square, back over the net to Doug's forehand. Doug hit it, harder this time. Andy ran, swung at it while running and hit it into the net.

Doug served to Andy's backhand. Andy got it back crosscourt. The return to his forehand was fast and in the corner away from him. He hustled like the dickens to get it. Doug hit hard and made him run back and forth, up to the net, then a lob over his head, and turning quickly chasing the ball way back to the baseline. After twenty minutes he was breathing hard, mouth open.

Doug was amused and laughed. "Getting tired, kid?"

"No. Hit some more."

Another fifteen minutes and Doug walked to the net.

"Take a break, kid. I'm tired, too. You run the heck out of a guy."

Andy was breathing through his teeth.

"What's your name?"

"Andy."

"I'm Doug Wixom."

"I know, I've watched you play."

"You're not bad for . . . How old are you?"

"Twelve."

"Well, you've got a lot of growing to do. I've seen you around here. You come down every day?"

"Every day I can. I'm practicing for the tournaments."

"Me too. Were you in the tournaments last year?"

"Yeah."

"Win?"

"I didn't come close even."

"Neither did I. I'm going to show them this year. Tough players at the club. Lot of tough players your age."

"Geez, don't I know it."

"You want to beat those kids, you'll need a lot of help. I can tell you a couple of things. If you'll listen."

"Sure. I'll listen."

"Okay, let's hit a few, Andy."

They hit the ball back and forth.

"Hold it," Doug told him, "You've got to stop and get set before you hit the ball. You can't hit the ball right if you're running. See, like this." Doug ran to the side, racquet pulled back as he moved, then stopped, feet in a solid position for a forehand stroke.

"See what I mean?"

"Yeah," Andy answered. "But I can't always get there fast enough."

"Run! Run! Keep your eyes on the ball. Watch what your opponent is doing. You've got to figure out where he's going to hit the ball. Then run and get to where the ball's going to be. You get set and ready. You just can't hit the ball right if you're running and swinging. Got it?"

"I'll try to remember."

"You have to remember!" Wixom flashed impatience. "You practice, practice, practice. All right. Let's get at it. Every time you don't do it right, I'll yell at you."

After eight outrageous shouts of protest by Doug, and returned screams of frustration by Andy, they were both plenty angry.

"Andy, you might not be the dumbest player around here, but you sure work at it."

"It's hard to do it right every time!"

"You're not trying hard enough."

"I am trying hard enough!"

"Then do it like I told you! Now get moving. Watch your feet! Run! Get there! Stop in position! Get set! Swing! Good God, Andy, you run like you had lead in your feet!"

"I can't run any faster!"

"You have to run faster!"

"I can't!"

"You can!"

A long stretch of silence past while they glared at each other. Then, a big grin crept over Doug's face. It started slowly and spread, the downward wrinkles curving upward like an animated clay face.

"C'mon, kid, let's go get a Coke."

It took longer for Andy's scowl to fade.

"Okay. Okay."

Doug put the coins in the machine, opened the first bottle and handed it to Andy.

"You'll be a good player someday," Doug said, smiling. "If you can last that long."

"I'll last," Andy said. "I'll last as long as I have to."

Doug laughed. "We'll see, won't we. We'll see."

Two evenings later, Andy hit again with Doug.

Doug yelled, "You're not doing what I told you!"

Andy stopped, looked at him defiantly. "I'm trying. You said hold the wrist stiff."

"Yes, but your arm at an angle. You can't hold your arm straight out and have control. Try it again. Here it comes."

Doug hit and Andy swung, not hard, but careful of the position of his arm. The ball went over, crosscourt, low over the net, dropping quickly. Doug ran for it, returned a high deep lob. "Good!" he cried out. "That's it."

A young man and a girl walked by at the end of the court on their way to number four court.

"Hey!" Doug shouted, everyone within a block hearing. "You don't just walk on a court like that when people are playing! What's the matter with going outside on the walk? You don't have to walk on the court when people are playing. How do you expect me to play when you're walking on the court?"

"Oh, sorry," the young man said, trying to smile it off. He hurried his pace, pulling the girl with him.

"Sure got a lot of idiots around this place. They don't know the first common sense rules of tennis! Just walk on the court when you're playing a match like it's the only thing to do!"

Andy wanted to laugh, but was afraid Doug might not like it.

"Well, are you ready? We'd better hurry before some more idiots take their evening stroll on our court!"

"I'm ready," Andy announced.

"Then pay attention! Watch your footwork. You're not stopping before you hit the ball. You've got to get there fast. Your racquet back and ready. Your feet in position. You can't get a proper swing if you're running. You've got to get there before the ball. Then Stop! Your feet in position. Swing. All right, now! Let's go! Watch your feet."

Andy watched his feet. He made several bad shots.

"Good God, kid! You just got worse!"

"I'm trying!"

"You've got to try harder!"

"I'll try harder!"

Doug went back to the fence, leaned his racquet against it. He took several deep breaths. Then put his hands on hips and squatted. "One-two. One-two. One-two. One-two." He stood up. Hands on hips. Touching his toes. "One-two-three. One-two-three. One-two-three. One-two-three." He took several deep breaths standing on his toes, reaching up high. He picked up his racquet again and looked at Andy.

He smiled. It was the smile of a friendly ogre.

"I'll tell you, Andy, if you weren't good, I wouldn't bother with you. Remember that. If you weren't good I wouldn't bother with you at all. Now, let's get at it again. Watch your footwork!"

"Okay," Andy answered. "Yes, Doug." He smiled, too. He felt pretty good now. He liked Doug. Doug was all right.

Finding someone to practice with every day was a problem. In the mornings and afternoons, few of the really good players were at the courts. In the evenings, when the weather was good, the courts were crowded. It was required to sign up in advance with Brian for a forty-five minute session.

Around Andy was beginning to form a small group of younger players who were quite serious about improving and becoming tournament competitors. There was Jim Hale, 14, Jerry Grant, 12, and Art Blaine, 14. Tom Yeates, the boy he had played doubles with the year before, had moved. And, there was Patty Sherry, 11. Patty belonged to the tennis club, but after Andy became a permanent inhabitant of the park, she spent many hours practicing there - Patty and her mother.

Mrs. Sherry was a non-player. It seemed her main purpose in life was to make Patty a champion. She was a largish woman, dressed well, and drove a blue Mercedes. Her entire conversation was Patty this and Patty that - and Patty's future tennis plans. She liked Andy because he hit the ball hard and was good practice for Patty.

Patty was a little overweight but quick with her feet

- when she wasn't in a lazy mood. For an eleven-year-old girl she had a hard serve. She liked to hit a fast serve and run up to the net, as she had seen the big boys do. In the back court she had trouble, she seemed unwilling to run after the ball if it was in an opposite corner.

"Patty skips rope for half an hour every day," her mother said. "She runs at least a mile . . . I hear that a twelve-year-old boy in Denver - whose ranked number one - wears weights on his ankles when he practices. That makes sense, doesn't it? When you take the weights off, you feel like you can fly. I'm going to get some for Patty . . . Good tennis players are good chess players. Did you know that, Andy? It's true. The Australians all play chess. Improves their strategy. That's the whole game - strategy. Outsmart your opponent. Make him do what you want him to do. . . And raisins . . . She eats raisins every day. Andy, you be sure and eat a lot of raisins. Every day. It'll improve your game."

Andy grinned, "Yes, ma'am."

It was June and time for the No Champs Tournament. It had been a long year of activity and many changes in Andy's life. He was eager for this tournament. He would play the club boys on his home ground and this time he was prepared, familiar with every foot of every court.

Jack parked near Brian's shack. Boys and girls were milling around waiting for court assignments. Jack and Andy knew most by name. Mrs. Groggin and Mrs. Banning were there to help Lee Hammel with his tournament. Andy carried his new racquet proudly, holding it up so everyone could see. Jack gave him the once-over: he was as well dressed as any kid on the courts. New white Wilson shorts at $5.00. White knit shirt $4.00. Converse tennis shoes $8.50. Heavy white socks $1.50. Jack was satisfied and smiled. It was certainly different than last year. Wasn't a boy from the club looked better than Andy.

Andy walked to the check-in table. "Hi, Brian. Hello, Mrs. Groggin. Hello, Mrs. Banning. Hello, Mr. Hammel."

Jack greeted the ladies. "Morning, Mrs. Groggin, Mrs. Banning."

"Hello, there Mr. Keller. So glad you could bring Andy. He sure looks nice."

"You always keep him dressed nice," Mrs. Banning said.

"It's part of the game," Jack added. "Now if he'll only win a trophy, it will be worth it."

"He will," Mrs. Banning said, in an confident tone. "Larry was telling me how much Andy had improved."

"He's got a long way to go."

"I've got to help Lee," Mrs. Groggin apologized. "Excuse me, please."

Jack sat on the bench with Mrs. Banning. They watched the boys go to their assigned courts. Andy to court seven and Larry to court three. Jack nodded towards Larry. "He's a fine boy."

Mrs. Banning smiled. He had been waiting for her to smile. She certainly was a fine looking woman.

"You don't have any children?"

"No," Jack answered, "only Andy. And he isn't really mine. His parents are divorced, no father in the home."

"I have three children. It . . . it isn't always enough."

143

Jack wasn't quite sure how far to go with this conversation.

"Where's Mr. Banning today?"

"Out of town. A business trip. He's very busy. Always very busy on business trips." She laughed, but it was an embarrassed laugh.

Jack watched the play on the courts. "Larry's playing well this morning. I don't think he'll have any trouble winning."

"He likes to win."

"Everyone likes to win. I haven't won for so long, I've almost forgotten what it's like."

"My husband always wins. Keeps him busy all the time. Busy, busy. On the go. To New York. Los Angeles. Always winning."

"He must be very happy."

"He's too busy winning to be happy."

"I'll have to think about that." Jack said, looking perplexed. "It's a new thought to me."

She smiled and their eyes met. It was such a warm smile, more than a friendly smile. It made him feel like he was floating. My God! he thought.

"I'll have Larry invite Andy to the house some weekend. They could practice on a court nearby."

He hoped this was more than small talk. Andy needed this kind of connection. She smiled again. He had a feeling he would do just about anything she asked him to do.

Andy and Larry won their matches. Jack spent the entire time talking with Carla Banning. It hadn't been the worst day in his life.

The next day, Andy lost in the first round of the 12

singles, but his first major victory in a tournament was in the second round of the fourteen. His opponent was Ken Walsh, a good player from the club. Walsh had the advantage of club lessons and a sixteen-year-old brother. The brother was good and in the second round of his age group.

Ken was a clown at times. While playing tournament matches, he liked to wear a New York Yankees baseball cap. Perhaps his biggest weakness was not taking the game seriously. This failing was something his family didn't understand. Members of tennis families must always take the game seriously.

Andy went on the attack from the first serve. He desperately wanted this match, and on this day everything he did was right. He hit tightly to the corners. He made only a few double-faults. He ran to the net at just the right times to hit the ball out of Ken's reach.

The first set ended 6-2. Ken panicked, realizing how much he had to lose, a member of the club, belonging to a tennis family, his brother a many-trophied winner; himself, last year's doubles' champion in two tournaments. Desperation.

Andy kept cool. What worked for him in the first set, now worked better in the second.

Jack sat on the edge of his seat watching, almost not believing it. He didn't say a word to Andy. Didn't need to. Between sets he hollered, "Keep it up. It's all yours."

Andy was simply playing over his head. It was one of those beautiful days to remember forever.

The second set ended 6-1. Andy was in the third round for the first time in his tennis life.

Andy's partner for the 14 doubles was Jim Hale, a good-looking blonde boy who was a half a foot taller than Andy. He played at the park and had been nothing better than a "batter" the year before. But, after practicing with Andy and getting in some doubles matches in the evenings against college players, he had improved more than he thought possible.

"I never got to play against men before you came down here," he said to Andy, at one afternoon practice. "I didn't know they'd play with kids."

"They will if you hit hard," Andy explained. "You've got to hit hard and run like crazy."

"I've never yet won a match in a tournament."

"If we get a good draw we could win the first round. I got terrible draws last year. Every time but once, I had to play one of those tennis club kids. I got wiped out."

"Me, too."

"Brian says since we've both been in tournaments last year we might get a good draw in the first round. If we get anyone but that club bunch, we've got a chance."

"How do they make that draw? Pick names out of a hat?"

"I don't know how they do it. But if you've got past the first round and played in a lot of tournaments, you get a better draw."

"They always put the park kids against someone from the club. We never have a chance."

"They think the park players are a bunch of dumb nobodies who don't know how to play and never will. That's why. I hope we can beat some of them."

"We can try," Andy said, meaning it.

The first round they were matched against two boys named Sorenson and Mitchell. Andy had never seen or heard of them. They were from a small suburban community in the southeast section of the valley and arrived early in two station wagons with their mothers and an assortment of relatives of all sizes and ages. They promptly brought out folding lawn chairs and noisily set them up alongside the court. The young ones were dispatched to the concession stand and returned with enormous bags of popcorn, some red and blue balloons, hot dogs and paper-cupped drinks for the entire group.

While warming up, Andy and Jim watched all this activity with apprehension.

"Hey," Andy joked, "looks like the circus is in town."

"Quiet, they might hear you," Jim said, nervously.

"I don't care, their stacking the sidelines to make us nervous. Just play like you're in the circus and the crowd loves us," Andy said, smiling.

"We're ready when you are," their opponents yelled.

"M or W?" Andy responded holding his racquet handle down on the court, ready to twirl it.

"M," shouted one of them.

Andy gave the racquet a spin. It wobbled, then slowly toppled over. Picking it up without looking, he pointed the end to the other boys.

"M. We'll serve."

"All right," Andy said to Jim. "You serve."

After losing the first two games, Andy and Jim settled down and won the set and the match 6-2, 6-1. There were a lot of close shots and disputed line calls, each side arguing throughout the match. Fortunately, the spectators kept out of it, unlike some little league baseball games, tennis audiences were better behaved.

"Thanks," Andy said, shaking hands at the net. "That was a good match, all right."

"If my mother wasn't here, I'd bust your head open," Sorenson said.

"Anytime," Andy responded. "Any time."

"Ah, You-suck Valdez."

Andy and Jim walked away without saying another word. They reported the score and went to the Coke machine. The rest of the afternoon Jim recounted every play to everyone he knew. To Andy, the victory was ugly. Soiled by bad sportsmanship and what he thought was another bad experience for no reason. The story of my life, he thought. At least, I did the right thing, cuz, I beat them at tennis, like Jack said, instead of punching them out.

The third round singles Andy was matched against Al Conrad.

"I'm going to beat that kid," Andy confidently told Jack.

"I hope so."

"Don't you think I can?"

"Not this year."

"You sure encourage a guy."

"It's simple facts. He's way ahead of you. Next year. Not this year."

"I want to beat him tomorrow."

"Play the best you can. Learn something."

"You always say, 'Learn something, learn something.'"

"Look, I want you to beat Al Conrad so bad I can taste it. Get some games from him tomorrow. That's all I ask now. Next year, you beat him. Someday, you'll beat him 6-0, 6-0 and the sky will fall in on the whole Conrad family. I can't stand that bunch. They've got shelves and shelves of trophies and still they want more. They come down to the park from their place in the clouds and play in this tournament and take trophies away from beginning players who really need one. The two boys play and take two. The girls take two. The old man and the son take another. And mama and daughter take another. Proud as a covey of peacocks, too. They beat the dumb-brains at the park and take half the trophies home so they can put up another shelf. Some people are like pigs working up to be hogs. For tennis people, they've got it made. The day you beat Al Conrad will be a big, big day for both of us."

"Tomorrow, I'll beat hell out of him."

"Don't swear like that."

"You always swear."

"I earned the right. You get my age, you'll have earned the right to swear. You don't get anything in this world without earning it."

"I'll try hard tomorrow."

"You bet. Try hard and learn something."

"You make it sound like school. Tennis is supposed to be a fun game."

"For those tennis club kids it's a fun game. For you it's serious business. That racquet will get you to the university someday. You'll get a scholarship playing tennis. An education. It may be the only way you'll get a college education."

149

"That's a long time from now."

"A long time? Six years. You know, kid, I could hold my breath for six years. That's how long six years really is."

It was an exciting, well-played match. Al took the first set 6-2. Andy came back to win the second 8-6 and was out playing the bigger stronger boy until he ran out of gas. Al won the third set 6-3.

Jack was pleased with the result. Even Andy didn't feel too bad about losing. "I'll get him next year. He isn't so tough. Next year."

In the second round of the doubles, Andy and Jim were outplayed all the way by Larry Banning and Al Conrad, 6-2, 6-2.

"You've come a long way in just one year," Jack told him proudly. "Just a year ago your first tournament was the No Champs. You haven't done badly at all."

"It sure seems like its been longer than a year. It seems like a lot longer than that."

Friday morning Jack stopped to see some customers and didn't arrive at the shop until about ten-thirty. A sheet of letterhead was thumb-tacked to the door.
JACK
I AM WITH MANUEL.
I WILL BE BACK IN HALF AN HOUR
 SOME GUYS JUMPED ME AND STOLE
MY BICYCLE.
WAIT HERE UNTIL I GET BACK
 - ANDY

Jack went into the shop, turned on the lights and jumped around the floor for a few minutes exterminating cockroaches. He inked up the offset press and wet down the dampener rollers. If that kid was running around all night, he thought, he'll hear about it. Getting beat up is the last thing we need. Losing the bike meant almost as much to Jack as it did to Andy. Whoever took it was going to be sorry, all right.

The door opened and slammed.

"Hi, Jack," Andy said. Manuel, who was a year younger, was with him. A quiet boy, Manual was willing to follow Andy anywhere. They both carried brown paper sacks. "We've been over to Woolworth's. They got cookies on special twenty cents a pound. Want some?" Andy opened his sack.

"You don't look hurt too bad. What happened? Where's the bike?"

"I was just going to tell you. It got stolen."

"That sure tells me a lot. Give me the details, and let's go find it."

"Two guys knocked me off it by the viaduct. They were waiting. They kicked me to keep me on the ground and then took off with my bike."

"You okay? Looks like you have a swollen cheek. Your legs and tennis arm hurt?"

"Yeah, my back is sore from the kicks and my knees and hands are scraped, but not bad. I've had worse beatings, that's for sure."

Jack was furious, "Animals, these guys knocking people off bikes. That's robbery! Who did it? Are they from your neighborhood? Give me some names."

"Oh, Johnny Carda for one and Ed Gardner."

"Sure, there's David Slater," Manuel piped up. "He

puts 'em up to it."

"You sure live in a great neighborhood. Anybody who doesn't do crimes?"

"Yeah me, and they don't live in my neighborhood. Don't go putting down the west side," Andy said hotly. "They go around all over the city stealing bikes in every neighborhood."

"Relax Andy," Jack commented. "As long as you're okay that's the first thing. I'd better call the cops. I'm so damn mad I want somebody to get it. That bike was like brand new and somebody's going to pay. One way or the other."

Jack called the police, "I want to report an assault and stolen bicycle."

"One moment, please."

"Hello, this is Sgt. McCall. Can I help you?"

"My name is Jack Keller . . . Keller K-E-L-L-E-R. I want to report an assault and they stole a kid's bicycle."

"Yes, sir. I'll turn you over to our bicycle division." Jack was placed on hold.

"Good morning, sir. This is Sgt. White."

"I'd like to report a stolen bicycle and an assault."

"Your name, sir?"

"Jack Keller. K-E-L-L-E-R. The boy was attacked this morning and they took his bike. It's a red Sears . . ."

"Excuse me, sir. The address."

"My address?"

"Where this happened."

Jack gave them him the information. No, he didn't have the serial number handy. He had it somewhere and would find it and call back.

"Ill prosecute this all the way," Jack told him. "I'll go with the officer who checks this out, and sign a complaint." Jack was ready to go. "How soon will an officer be here to do something about this?"

"We have a limited number of men available for the juvenile division and our bicycle men won't be in until Monday."

"Bicycle men? This is a robbery. The boy was knocked of his bike and beaten!"

"Was there serious bodily injury that required hospitalization?"

"No, he's right here next to me, but he is hurting."

"Sir, this goes to our bicycle men. Monday they'll get on it."

"Monday? This is Friday. It'll be too late."

"It's the best we can do. The bicycle men only work part-time in the mornings. Monday morning at nine?"

"Monday morning. All right."

He wanted to bang the phone down but didn't. "How do you like that? Monday! Can't do anything until Monday."

"Geez, I'll never get it back," Andy looked down. "We can't do anything until Monday?"

"I don't know. We could go chasing around where those boys live. But if they find out we're after them, they won't have anything around when the cops get there. They could get rid of it piece by piece. We'd never see any of it again."

"You think they'll wreck it and tear it apart?"

"You know they will. They can sell the parts. They won't leave it alone."

"I want my bike!" Andy hollered. "I can't get along without wheels. How'd you like it if your car was stolen . . . and you had to ride the dumb bus or walk?"

"We'll wait until Monday. The cops know how to handle this. I've never been mixed up with crooks and thieves before. When I was your age, I never had a bike. I had to walk everywhere."

"It isn't my fault it was stolen."

"I didn't say it was. It just happened, that's all. Those guys will pay, I guarantee it."

"Johnny Carda's been in the reform school twice," Manuel said.

"I guess he learned a trade while he was there. How to make a living robbing people. Monday, we'll get them. If I have to call the Chief of Police and the Mayor and the Police Commissioner. Monday!"

"You'll get it back for me," Andy added, hopefully. "I know you will."

Monday morning, Jack answered the phone.

"Good morning, sir, this is Officer Middleton. My partner and I have been assigned to work on this battery and bicycle theft you reported. Could we see you at nine?"

"Sure can. I'll go with you if you're going to follow this through."

"We'd appreciate any help you can give, Mr. Keller. Shall we come over to your shop?"

"I'll be out in front of the Capitol Theatre. Right by the alley. Okay?"

"That's fine, Mr. Keller. In ten minutes."

Jack phoned Andy and told him to wait at his house. If the officers wanted to talk to him, they'd be able to find him. Out front, a blue car with no insignia made a turn into the alley and stopped. The man driving wore a gray suit and no hat. He was young and slender and looked like a junior executive.

"I'm Officer Middleton. Mr. Keller?" He held out his hand.

"Glad to meet you. I'm ready. I'll go with you. I want that bike back as soon as possible."

"So do we, Mr. Keller. Get in the back."

Jack got in and as they drove, he started to give them the details.

The other young fellow, in a brown suit, introduced himself. "I'm Officer Carter, Mr. Keller." They shook hands. "Do you know who did this? Have any names?"

"I've got names. Johnny Carda, Ed Gardner, David Slater."

"Oh, David and Johnny Carda," Middleton said. "They just got out of the State Industrial School."

"We've had problems with them before," Carter added. "The other boy is a friend. We've had problems with all of them."

"Let's go see Johnny first."

"His mother will love us," Carter said.

They drove across the tracks and into an older residential area. Some of the houses were well kept, with green lawns bordered by flowers and shrubs. Some were shabby with broken windows, garbage everywhere, knee high weeds and broken down cars.

They stopped in front of a red brick house with a small wood-fenced yard and grass that needed cutting. A girl about five-years-old was in the yard, wearing a faded flower-designed dress and no shoes. She was bouncing a ball. When she saw them get out of the car, she disappeared around the back of the house.

"You talk to her," Carter said. "I did it last time. It's your turn."

"I had a feeling this wasn't going to be my day," Middleton replied. He smiled at Jack. "Don't worry. You don't need to say anything. What we need you for is to identify the bike. Positive identification is what we need. You can stay in the car if you like."

"I'll go with you," Jack said. "I've never done this before."

"Well, for you, it's a day to remember," Carter said, skeptically.

Jack followed them through the gate to the wood porch, the steps creaking under their feet. Middleton pushed a button by the door.

A low growl come from inside and suddenly the huge head of an enormous coal black dog was in front of them, only the flimsy screen door keeping them apart. The dog snarled a warning and bared a row of sharp teeth.

The three of them gave a start and froze. "Don't move," Middleton said quietly. "I don't think he's dangerous."

"He could bite your leg off without half trying," Carter joked, nervously.

"Is that a dog or a wolf?" Jack asked. He didn't move, just breathing very quietly.

"Get away from there, Jubo!" A woman's shrill voice shouted. "Come back here, now, you Jubo. Now!"

The dog growled again, then reluctantly moved

away from the door.

"Officers Middleton and Carter, ma'am." They showed their badges.

"I know you two. You been here before. Why do you keep coming back here?"

"We'd like to talk to Johnny."

"What do you want with Johnny? You keep after him all the time. Can't you let that boy alone? He hasn't done anything. He is doing good since he got out. You just keep persecuting that boy."

"We'd like to talk to him, Mrs. Carda," Middleton said. "All we want is just to see him and talk to him."

"He's not here. You're always persecuting that boy. Why don't you leave him alone?"

Middleton sighed. "We'd sure like to, Mrs. Carda. But we've got a problem with Johnny."

"What's that?"

"He won't give us the chance to leave him alone."

Suddenly Jack felt something wet on his leg, then he heard the water spraying. All three of them felt the water. Turning, they found the five-year-old standing on the lawn with the hose. She was pointing it at them and smiling as if it were a joke. She laughed like it was sure fun.

They made a fast run for the car. The little girl tried to reach them with the hose. Jubo started barking. Mrs. Carda screamed, "Why don't you lousy cops stop persecuting my boy? He never does anything, but you cops got nothing else to do but persecute my boy."

Middleton gunned the car away from the curb.

"This happen every day?" Jack asked, squeezing some of the water out the legs of his pants.

157

"Only every other day," Carter answered.

Two blocks away they pulled up at a green painted frame house with a picket fence and a neatly kept yard. A boy about sixteen sat on the porch.

Getting out, Middleton waved at the boy, "Hi, Ed."

The boy looked at him glumly, didn't say anything.

Middleton opened the gate cautiously. There was no sign of a dog. Jack felt foolish standing there with wet pants.

"This is ridiculous," Carter said, smoothing his hands along his pant-legs, water dripping on his shoes.

"Ed, you seen Johnny today?"

"Not today."

"Okay. You know where he is?"

"I haven't seen him today or yesterday, either."

"You got a bike today, Ed?"

"Why?"

"We want to see it. You can bring it out and let us look at it or we can get a warrant."

"I've got a bike. It's my own bike."

"Get it."

The boy reluctantly went around the side of the house. Carter followed. They reappeared with Ed wheeling a nondescript bike, green frame.

"That's the front wheel," Jack said, excitedly. "There's a mark on the rim I put on with a file. The back wheels got the same mark. This is the front wheel, all right."

"Anything else?"

"The seat. Looks exactly like the one on Andy's bike. Could be the same kind. I didn't mark it."

"Take the wheel and the seat off, Ed," Middleton

told him.

"This is my bike!" the boy protested.

"Take the wheel and seat off."

The boy grumbled and then took a small crescent wrench from his pocket, upended the bike, loosened the nuts.

"He's pretty good at that," Jack said.

"Oh, he's had a little experience," Carter answered.

"I don't know what you guys are talking about," the boy said. "I bought this wheel and the seat. I paid for them."

"Buy them from Johnny?"

"Yes."

"When?"

"Saturday. I bought them Saturday."

Jack took the front wheel and the seat. Carter unlocked the trunk and put them inside. They climbed in and drove away.

"We going to pick up the bike piece by piece?" Jack asked.

"Could be. We've got those other two boys to check out."

"This is sure a hell of a thing," Jack said. "I bought that boy this bike. We went down to Sears and he picked out the one he wanted. A beautiful candy apple red bike with chrome rims, and then I got those high handlebars for him and a light and an electric horn. I never had a new bike when I was a kid. I bought it for Andy. I guess it was kind of making up for it, never having a new one myself, buying him the new bike. It sure hits me in the guts having this happen."

"You're lucky it's only a bike dismantled . . . worse things happen in this area to kids, believe me."

"I know but money is scarce and buying that bike set me back because . . . "

Middleton interrupted, "Well, Mr. Keller - the boy was knocked off his bike and kicked, no broken bones or serious injuries, count your blessings. Some of these hoodlums are known for hurting people not just stealing."

"Right. Sometimes I forget the important things. The kid is tough. He bends back like twisted plastic and I lose sight of the damage that was inflicted. I'm sorry for obsessing over the bike."

"Tell it to the kid," Middleton said sharply, ending the discussion.

After a short drive, they stopped at a two-story, faded-yellow brick house. The front yard was dirt bordered with high weeds.

"I hate coming here," Carter said. "I feel so damn sorry for these people. They've had so much bad luck you wouldn't believe it. And the boy, David, sure doesn't make things any better."

"I guess everybody in this neighborhood has bad luck," Middleton added. "I hope he doesn't have anything to do with this."

"I don't want to cause any boy trouble," Jack said, feeling sorry now. "I just want the bike."

"Don't go back on us now, Mr. Keller," Middleton told him. "You told us you'd go all the way on this case. We find the boys who hit and stole the bike, you've got to sign a complaint like you said."

Jack sighed. "Sure, sure. I know it. All the way."

The path led them through a disarray of wooden boxes and empty buckets and partly filled cans of paint and rusty auto parts and burlap sacks filled with old bottles and broken furniture to the back of the house.

When she heard them she turned and smiled. Her face had an exhausted look but her smile was friendly.

"Oh, hello there, Mr. Middleton. And you, Mr. Carter. How are you?"

"Good morning, Mrs. Slater," Middleton said, politely. "It's a nice morning, isn't it?"

"Oh, yes. I love it when it's like this. All cool and the sky so clear - and the birds singing as if it was almost the resurrection. It's a lovely morning. I suppose you're looking for David?" The smile faded.

"We'd like to talk to him, Mrs. Slater."

"Mr. Middleton, I really wish you would talk to him. Talk some sense into him. He needs someone to help him."

"I've tried, Mrs. Slater. Believe me, I've tried. I don't want that boy in trouble any more than you do. Our job is to prevent trouble. We have a hard time convincing people of that. But it's true. We're not going to make trouble for David."

She tried a smile again, but it didn't come. "He's in the basement. I'll send him up." She turned and went inside.

"Look around," Middleton said to Carter. "Look in that shed over there."

"Okay, but we've never found anything here."

Mrs. Slater returned with the boy following. He walked the institutional strut, picking it up in reform school. He was about fifteen now and his face wore a permanent scowl. He stared at the officers, defiantly.

"Hi, David," Middleton greeted him. "Come out to the car. We want to talk to you."

161

"What for?"

"Come out to the car."

Middleton, the boy and Jack went to the car. Carter continued his investigation of the back yard.

Middleton opened the back door, "Get in. We'll talk."

"Where you taking me?"

"Get in."

Middleton nodded at Jack and he got in the back seat, too. The boy moved away as far as he could. Middleton got in on the driver's side.

"We're looking for bikes, David."

"I don't know nuttin about bikes. I don't even got one."

"Where's Johnny Carda today?"

"I don't know."

"David, someone hit and stole a bike from Andy Valdez. Now you know Andy and his brother James. Right?"

"Yeah, we use to sell papers togedder. Andy's a chump wit out his brotherr."

"James did you a big favor one time. Seems like he helped you out one day when you got jumped by four of the Jensen boys. You might have got killed that day if James hadn't helped you. That's the way I heard the story. Did it happen that way, David?"

"Maybe. You guys hear lots of things."

"James is a pretty tough fighter. . . A nice kid and his brother's a nice kid and they're good people to have for friends. Sometimes a guy needs all the friends he can get. James wouldn't like it a bit if he knew you stole his brother's bike."

"Andy's not my friend anyways . . . and James he's psycho, he hit you wit a pipe when he fights . . . go get him! I didn't take nuttin man . . . it was Johnny!"

"That's what I figured. You've got enough problems without robbing people for bikes. Been a lot of bikes stolen lately around here.

"Now Mr. Keller is a friend of the Valdez family and he's going to make it mighty tough for whoever hits Andy. We don't want you mixed up in this, if you didn't have anything to do with it. You help us and we'll help you. Isn't that right, Mr. Keller?"

"Absolutely," Jack said. "I'm not interested in making trouble for anyone who didn't have anything to do with this."

"What you want me to do?" David asked, unhappy about the whole business.

"We don't seem to be able to find any of those bikes or even the parts. Maybe you might have an idea where we could find something."

David hesitated. He glanced at Jack, looked out the window, bit his lip.

Carter came around the house to the front yard, gave it a quick inspection, and got in the car. "Nothing, nothing," he reported.

"Where to, David?" Middleton turned and looked at David.

"Go to the big dirt overpass where the freeway being built. It's just dirt but you can git up on top."

Middleton drove to a new concrete overpass recently completed except for the paving of the new freeway

163

approach. It was rough going as they maneuvered around ditches and ruts and piles of gravel and sand until they got to the overpass.

"On top here?" Middleton asked.

Slater nodded in the direction of the overpass.

"Keller, you come with me."

They walked about sixty feet, then saw something bright red gleaming in the sun.

Jack hurried to the frame laying in the dirt. "This isn't it."

"A Raleigh," Middleton said, picking it up. "I know this one." He upended it. "Number filed, but there are marks on the back here. Three notches. I know this one. Brand new. The kid had it two days. Well, let's go on. Might be some more."

They continued until they found two out of shape wheels, a worn seat, some rusty handlebars, but nothing of Andy's bike. Jack and Middleton gathered them up.

"These will clear up a few cases. Don't tell us who stole them, but it helps."

"I don't see how," Jack said, confused. "Just a bunch of parts of bikes."

"We take these around and ask questions. Sometimes, we get the answers we need."

At the police car they put the parts in the trunk.

"David's been telling me about Andy's bike," Carter said. "It was Johnny Carda, all right."

"Were you with him, David?"

"No. But he brung the bike to my place Saturday. He ditn't know it was Andy. He says he took the bike from a white-boy dressed in white clothes. He lie cuz he say he don't know Andy but he did."

"What happened to the bike?"

"I don't know. He ditn't want no trouble wit James Valdez bout it. I woodn't let him leave it wit me. He took it somewhere. I ain't saw him since Saturday."

"Okay, David, right now we're going to believe you. And tomorrow I want to believe you. And the day after."

At David's house, the boy got out.

"David," Middleton started, "I don't ever want to see you again except maybe in church. Maybe you could stop wasting time with Johnny Carda and wise up and get a job and help your mother. She's been damn good to you for a long time. Maybe you're grown-up enough now to return the favor. How about it?"

The boy didn't say anything. He half-smiled, shrugged and walked away.

"I've got a notion where the bike might be right now," Middleton said, and drove to Andy's house. When the car pulled up, Andy came running out.

"Jack, Jack! I got my bike back!"

"What happened? How?"

"We went to the store and when we got back I had to put the garbage can out, and the bike was in the alley, leaning up against the fence." Andy was excited and talked fast. "Jack, it's sure a mess. It's all scratched and the high handlebars are gone. And, the electric horn. And, it's got a different front wheel and a beat up seat. It's sure a mess, Jack."

"We've got the front wheel and the seat," Jack said.

"Let's look at it," Middleton said.

"Officer's Middleton and Carter, this is Andy."

"Hi."

"Hi, Andy. Let's take a look."

The bike was in the back yard. Jack winced. It sure wasn't the beautiful bike they bought from Sears. The candy apple red paint was scratched and scraped.

"Why'd he bring it back?" Jack asked.

"I'm just guessing," Middleton said. "Maybe he didn't want James and Andy on him. Maybe he thought it over and decided to bring it back, hoping that would end it. Maybe he heard about you going with us on this chase and figured you might cause more trouble than we would."

"Why is it so beat up?"

"Sometimes a stolen bike is stripped and the frame taken down to the railroad yard and thrown into an empty coal car. The frame can be traced but it's not so easy to identify the wheels and other parts. Maybe this bike was thrown into a car to get rid of the whole thing and then maybe whoever stole it decided to bring it back. He put on another front wheel and seat and those old handlebars." He scratched his head. "Now this is only a lot of guessing, you know."

"You seem positive it was Johnny Carda."

"No. That's another maybe. When we talk to him he can tell us all about it.

"Would you like us to take you back to your shop, Keller? We'll be trying to locate Johnny with what time we've got left today. You've probably got business to take care of."

"Well, if you don't need me. I should get back."

"Can I go uptown with you?" Andy asked.

"Hurry if you want to go with us."

Andy hurried.

"Nice kid," Carter said.

"The best," Jack answered. "He used to sell papers on the corner near my shop. I got acquainted with him and he decided he'd rather work for me, running errands, cleaning up, things like that. I'm divorced, no kids. It can be lonesome working by yourself. To me, that boy is the sun and the moon."

"There's one thing about Andy we can be pretty sure of," Middleton offered.

"What's that?"

"He's one of the lucky ones. Most of these westside boys don't have people to show them the right way. He's a lucky one."

The time came when Jack was no match for Andy. It was actually a gradual process, but the awareness came suddenly to Jack on an evening when Andy became hotly impatient.

"Hit it harder!" Andy yelled.

"I'm hitting it hard!" Jack said.

"You're not hitting it hard enough!"

Jack hit the ball as hard as he could. Out. The second one out, too.

"Oh, geez! I can't get any practice this way!"

Andy hit the ball to the corner away from Jack. Jack ran but couldn't push his legs harder. The next ball went to the other corner. He couldn't touch it.

"Run! Run! Run!" Andy hollered.

Damn smart kid, Jack grumbled. Getting too good now. Getting big ideas he's too good now.

The ball whizzed over the net and dropped in front of him, so fast he couldn't move or get the racquet to it. It hit him in the side and felt like a rock.

"Look out, now!" Jack said. "Don't act like a smart-aleck!"

Andy made a face. "How can I get any practice when you just stand there?"

Jack picked up the balls to serve. His side hurt. It was an effort to reach up and swing. He hit the ball, not hard, but placed it exactly where he wanted it, at a sharp angle, just over the net, dropping inside the line.

Andy scrambled, swung desperately, got the ball with the wood weakly, not enough to get it back. The next serve was straight down the center line, fast, just inside and low. 30-Love.

Andy got the next serve back. Jack hit it deep, keeping Andy to the back of the court. Back it came, Jack half way up. He sliced it sharply. The ball went over in a spinning arc, dropping almost straight down close to the net. Andy got it on the second bounce. 40-Love. The last serve was better than the first, dropping close to the net and just ticking inside the line.

Jack grinned. "What's the matter, kid? Can't run fast enough? C'mon, give me some competition."

Andy flared. He hit the balls as hard as he could into the back fence. He then threw his racquet into the net.

Jack lost the next game and the set.

Andy worked off his hotheadedness. "I'm sorry," he said. "I didn't mean to get so mad."

Jack's feelings were hurt. "You'd better learn to control that Spanish hot head. You can't play right when you're blowing a fuse."

Andy laughed. "I know. Let's get out of here and get

something to eat. We can come back later."

Jack had a silly desire to sulk.

"Don't be mad," Andy told him, "I'm just a dumb ignorant kid."

"Yeah. Let's go eat," Jack said.

Wednesday afternoon Mike Franchetti came into the shop. He was wearing a new expensive-looking blue suit, white shirt, blue tie, blue hat. The cigar he was smoking, now half gone, smelled like something very, very expensive.

"Hi, Jack. How's it going?"

"Hi, Mike. Haven't seen you lately."

"Busy as hell on a couple of new cases."

"You look like a prosperous new car dealer. New suit?"

"My wife made me buy it. Said if I was going to do high class business I had to look high class. I need some printing."

"This is the place. What is it?"

Mike held out some envelopes and letter-sized paper.

"Letterhead with this letter printed on it. I want the letterhead and envelopes two-color this time. Make the letter in black. So it looks like a typewriter, you know."

"Okay. I'll run it a bit grayish to match your typewriter. You need a new ribbon, but I can match this. How about the red? Bright red?"

"Yeah. Like that postcard you did. Like that. And a good dark blue.

This purple blue okay? Looks good with bright red."

"Sure."

"Want to see a proof?"

"Phone me. If I can make it, I'll look at it. These are in kind of a hurry."

"Rush-rush. How about lunch, Mike. Got time?"

Mike checked his watch. "Got an appointment at one-thirty. Sure, if you can go now."

"I can. Where? My turn to buy. Any place you like."

"No, I'll buy. I picked up a good pay last week. I know, I told you I'd take you to that place down the street, The Starlite. Go-Go girls with lunch."

"All right. I haven't had Go-Go girls with lunch yet."

"These girls are real wild for this town. I don't think they'll be there long. Someone will close them down one of these days."

"Yeah. Probably."

"How's the boy getting along with the tennis?"

"Real good this year. Working hard and getting better all the time."

"You spend a lot of time on that kid. You know, Jack, you should have married a nice Italian girl and had half a dozen kids. Italian girls make the best wives. Good cooks, lots of loving and lots of kids. The only way to live, Jack."

"Don't I know it. How's your boy doing in the Little League?"

"Man, you should have seen him make a catch Saturday. He's the littlest guy on the team and this ball goes up so high it almost disappears and then down it comes in left field and there he is all alone trying to find it. He catches it like Willie Mays. Man, everyone stood up and cheered. It was the greatest."

"Kids are a lot of fun," Jack agreed. "Well, if you've

got an appointment, we better go. How's the weather?"

"Hot. You don't need a coat. I have to wear mine every time I go out."

"Is the Starlite a coat place?"

"They don't care what you wear."

"That's my place, all right. Everything I've got has ink on it. I look like a bum."

"You wouldn't win any prizes for being the best-dressed."

"I haven't won any prizes for being the worst dressed."

"I didn't know they were giving them."

"Sure. Why not?"

Out in the alley they walked to Second South.

"You collect anything from Stern Jewelry yet?"

"Just a promise."

"That's what they gave me. Want me to call them again?"

"I told them I had turned the account over to you. I thought it would stir them up."

"I'll call tomorrow and stir them up. We'd better get some money out of them before they go broke. You let that account go too long, Jack. You're just too damn easy going with people like that."

"I hate to make trouble. I hate to have to beg people to pay me money they owe me."

"But the ones you owe don't care about that now, do they?"

"They don't. Mike, some days it's sure a rat race."

"You've just got to keep ahead of the rats, that's all."

"There must be a better way of making a living."

"The only solution, Jack. Be born rich."

After a sweaty day at the print shop, one of those days when everything was a rush and everything seemed to go wrong, Jack was exhausted. The phone rang every few minutes with someone calling about a past due bill, and the offset press gave him trouble time and again. There never seemed to be enough money to go around. This kind of day would never end unless Jack stopped it.

Andy practiced at the park. Sometime after six o'clock Jack pulled the switch, turned off the lights and locked all the doors. He liked to be at the courts in the evening when the sun was setting and a breeze made it cool. On the best nights every one they knew, all the aficionados, were there. Doug and Jim and Fred and Gary and Patty Sherry and Mrs. Sherry. And, the college people, Ron and Dave and Sarah and Carol, and friends of Andy's, the few who could stay late at the park. Frank and his daughter, Louise, were always fun to play doubles with, and some nights Jack and Andy could win easily, but other nights they really got taken.   During the daytime, Andy practiced, but evening tennis was a fun game.

Jack's playing time was regulated by how tired he was. He usually could go a couple of sets of doubles, with Andy doing all the running. He watched, visited and rested many evening. Jack was a good listener so conversation always seemed to find him .

After sunset, when the hottest part of the day cooled, the park courts were as pleasant a place that could ever be found. The air was gently scented from the flower beds and tree blossoms. The park was populated with giant trees making it an urban forest. There was night swimming at the pool and next to it was a large playground and picnic area. Laughter rose up from the amusement rides, and the carousel music wafted in and out all the way to the tennis court. The refreshment stand offered good-tasting hamburgers and fries.

Twice a week at the historic bandstand, a big band played or children performed dance recitals, or cowboy-attired square dancers do-se-doed. Some nights, they set up a projector and played movies, but nearly every night during the summer months, something was happening.

Next to the bandstand sat a fairly large lake, with islands inhabited by ducks and geese and rabbits. A paddle-wheel boat circled the lake and along the shoreline boys fished for carp, suckers and catfish. The water reflected the sunset and later the street lamps. At sunset, the birds in the Aviary sang out and filled the entire park with an exotic sound. On the best nights, a full moon rose just above the high Wasatch Mountains to the east and the park bathed in its soft magical light. It was all so wonderful and filled with friendly people and lovely places to explore. Andy sometimes leaned on the fence and let his eyes and heart and soul fill up with the liveliness of the night. These were good times to be alive at the park.

On this particular night, Andy was bugging Brian. "Can't you get me a court? Jim's here tonight. We need to get in a lot of practice. He can only play at night. Look at some of those guys out there. They run around like butterfly catchers. Some of them have been chasing and swatting air for hours. Tell them their time's up."

Brian shrugged, "Everybody gets their turn."

"Ah, Brian!"

"You've got a court in half an hour."

Tourists were also at the park at night for tennis. Some checked the yellow pages first and, of course, saw the tennis club listing and went to it. They were turned down. "Private club. Only by invitation - if you know a member."

One man from New York, a slender, tanned and well dressed fellow arrived at the courts. He carried a steel racquet, unopened can of balls, and held his racquet like he knew what it was all about. He arrived in a new T-Bird and told Brian, "I've been up to the club. I got the message you have to have a speaking acquaintance with Jesus Christ to play there. Any chance I can get a decent match here?"

"I think so. Carl Johnson is around somewhere. He goes to the University. He's quite good. There he is, by number two court. The fellow with the black hair. I'll sign you up a court. Let's see. Number seven in fifteen minutes."

"Thanks, fella. It's nice to have places like this where an out-of-towner can get a game without a gold card."

After the man left, Andy asked, "Who's he, Brian? He looks like a tough player."

"Some guy from New York. A tourist, I guess."

"I'd like to play him. I never played anyone from New York."

"He's going to ask Carl to play. They'll be on seven. Maybe he'd play you tomorrow. He said he wants to get in some games."

Andy waited then went over to seven. Carl and the man were warming up. He had a good forehand and a fair backhand. He moved with grace and quickness. He had good control of the ball.

When he came close, Andy said, "Hello, Brian said you needed someone to play."

"I've got a match now, sorry."

"I mean maybe tomorrow. Brian said you were from New York."

"That's right, here for a few days on business. You play tough?"

The man smiled and turned to Carl "Hey, Carl, you know this kid?"

"Yeah, sure."

"He a good player?"

"He'll give you a match."

"Okay, kid. What's your name?"

"Andy Valdez."

"I'm Mark Collins. How about two o'clock tomorrow?"

"You bet."

"Don't forget now. And don't be late."

"I'll be here. You bet. I've never played anyone from New York."

"I didn't know it was such a great honor. You know, I never heard of Salt Lake City until I had to make a trip here."

"I don't know where New York is, either."

"Ah, come on!" The man laughed.

"Well . . . " Andy started, waving to the east, "it's that way somewhere . . . three or four or five thousand miles."

"You're right. It's that way somewhere. Okay, tomorrow at two."

"See you then," Andy said, satisfied.

Andy went back to Brian's shack. "I'm going to play that guy from New York tomorrow."

"Play tough," Brian said.

When he saw Jack he told him, "I'm going to play a guy from New York tomorrow. At two. Can you bring me?"

"Yes. Good player?"

"He looks real tough. Got everything new. Came in that new T-Bird over there. He's playing Carl now. Never played anyone from New York before, have I?"

"Not unless they kept it a secret. Some people like to keep it a secret where they came from. But not people from New York. They tell you right off, 'I'm from New York, I'm from New York.' Like they were doing you a favor."

The second week of July started the Public Parks Tournament. Andy won easily in the first and second singles rounds. In the third round, Jack watched Andy blow four straight games. Andy's serve. He grinned and waved his racquet at Jack. Jack stared glumly.

Come to life, Jack said, to himself. No coaching during the match. Get in there and play!

Andy aced the first serve. Another. Another. Double-fault. Won the game with and ace. 1-4. Andy waved his racquet again at Jack. Big smile.

Jack wanted to throw something. Fooling around in a third round quarterfinal match.

Andy lost the next game. 1-5.

Jack groaned and walked away. He couldn't watch. I'll tell him, he repeated to himself, I'll sure tell him!

At court number 4, Art Gordon watched his son, Rick.

"How's it go, Art?"

"I don't know what's the matter is with him today." He said, shaking his head. "Playing like he doesn't know what's going on."

"What's the score?"

"He's down two-five. Just fooling around. Like he didn't care whether he wins or loses." He turned and looked at Jack, "How's Andy doing?"

"Playing like he's got rocks in his head. Lost the first set, I guess. I couldn't watch any more."

Rick served a smash ball into the corner out of reach. Rick was fourteen, a good-looking blonde boy. On the court, he moved gracefully. He had a beautiful forehand, a strong backhand, a power serve. He was the kind of player who gave the impression he could be great if he would just try a little harder. Or practice more often. Or take the game a little more seriously. Or something.

Rick lost the next point. 30-all. Putting power into the serve, he aced it.

"Terrific serve," Jack said.

Art grunted.

Rick lost the next point on a line-drive passed him.

"Lazy, lazy!" Art exclaimed. "He doesn't seem to want to move."

Deuce. The first serve out. The second returned to his backhand.

Rick returned to backhand. Down the side to his forehand. He made a tremendous swing back down the line, barely touching inside the corner.

"Good shot!" Jack hollered.

Rick prepared to serve. He tossed it up, a smashing

177

down stroke, the ball shot in - couldn't be touched by the other player. Rick's game.

"He'll snap out of it," Jack offered. "He's playing great now."

Art admitted, "I guess it means more to me than it does to Rick. I want that boy to be a champion so bad. I'd give my right arm. Greatest thing in the world to me if he'd be ranked number one in the Intermountain area."

Jack returned to Andy's court. Andy was still acting like it was a holiday. He glared at his opponent and grinned at the spectators. Between shots he twirled his racquet with a one-finger trick.

"Good shot!" he shouted, at everything he missed.

Andy was interesting to watch. He had something. Class, charm, personality. A magnetism that attracted attention. Jack couldn't name it, but it was there. Fine. But it didn't win matches.

"What's the score?" he asked a boy nearby.

Andy lost the first set. I don't know what it is now."

Jack turned and walked away. Damn, just fooling around. Just throwing it away. He couldn't watch any longer. I'll tell him something, all right, you just wait.

He walked around the park more than once, avoiding the courts, not wanting to watch Andy lose. I'll tell that fool kid something!

When he finally returned, Andy was smiling and talking to friends.

"I won," Andy announced, proudly. "Where'd you go?"

"I watched you fooling around and losing the first set. You played like an idiot. I couldn't take it."

"You know I'm a slow starter. I took him six-0, six-one the next sets. Why didn't you stay? I knew I was going to beat him."

"You knew!" Jack put his hands on his hips, what can I do with this kid?

"Did you have to make it a tough match?" Jack asked, exasperated. "Couldn't you just take the first set and finish it off?"

"It was fun. I knew I was going to beat him. It made him feel good winning the first set. His parents were watching. He's a nice kid."

"Nice kid, nice kid! Listen, you go in and win six-0, six-0. I don't care how nice the kid is you're playing."

Andy changed the subject, "Rick won in three sets. He had a tough match."

"That'll make his father feel better," Jack said, trying to control himself.

"I'm hungry. Let's get out of here and go eat." He smiled shyly at his mentor, "Okay, Jack?"

The boy was happy about winning. This was the furthest he had ever made it in a tournament. The semifinals. Not bad.

Jack was happy.

The day before the first round of the 14 doubles, his partner, Jim Hale, sprained an ankle swimming in the park pool. It wasn't serious but it was too painful for him to play.

"What do I do now, Jack?" Andy asked. "I'm not going to play with just anybody."

"All right, lets get someone at the club. Who isn't in the doubles?"

"Rick? I don't think he is."

"Phone him."

"What if he doesn't want to?"

"You don't know until you ask him."

"His parents might not want him to play with me."

"Oh, come on. He isn't that much better than you. You and Rick would have a terrific chance of winning. And, his parents sure wouldn't object to his getting another trophy."

"Well, all right. We'd have a good chance, wouldn't we?"

"Sure would."

Andy dialed.

"Hello, is Rick there? This is Andy Valdez . . . Yes . . . He isn't? Oh . . . I was wondering if he wanted to be my partner in the doubles tournament? My partner sprained his ankle . . . I need someone tomorrow morning . . . Yes, sure . . . You'll tell him? Yes, at eleven tomorrow . . . All right, I'll see him . . . Thanks, Mrs. Gordon. Goodbye."

Big smile.

"Okay?" Jack asked.

"Okay! It was his mother. She said Rick would be glad to be in the doubles with me."

"If he wasn't there, how would she know?"

"I don't know, Jack. She said she was glad I called and he would be glad to play with me. She will bring him."

"That was easy."

"I didn't think they'd want him to."

"Listen, Andy." Jack said in a serious tone, "I don't want you to ever forget, you're just as good as they are. Just as good as Rick and his family and anyone else at the tennis club."

"You say that but it isn't easy believing it all the time. They've got lots of money and big houses and new cars - all kinds of things we don't have. The kids call me names behind my back."

A twinge of emotion welled up, "Well, that's a hard argument, Andy. We've got three good things, though."

"What three?"

"Faith, hope and guts. They win a lot of ball games."

"I don't know when you're kidding and when you're not."

"I'm not kidding." Jack was proud of Andy. "Who you playing tomorrow?"

"Don't know them. Ted Brown and Ron Smith."

"You won't have any trouble - first round."

"I sure hope we win this, Jack. Geez, I'd like to get a trophy. All the time I've been playing - a year now - I haven't got a trophy."

"You don't want it more than I do. I'm glad you'll be playing with Rick. He's a fighter. You'll have to hustle."

"I will. I'd sure hate it if we lost on account of me playing badly. He'd never forget it - neither would his parents. Not to mention the club would never forget it."

"You know it!"

"Maybe I shouldn't have called."

"You're sweating it now. Getting chicken?"

"I just hope I'm playing good tomorrow. Maybe I ought to practice more tonight."

"You've had enough tennis for today. Tournaments are tough, mentally and physically. You'd better get all the sleep you can."

"I'm hungry."

"Lets go, then. You have steak, salad and milk. Then home and sleep."

"It's early, every one will be there." He started worrying. I hope no one is mad or fighting."

"They will understand you're in a tournament, right? In training and needing rest and quiet."

"Will you tell them Jack?"

"I'll tell your mother that the TV will be off and everyone has to talk in whispers. No yelling, hitting or fighting. Quiet as kittens. How does that sound?"

"Jack, you don't know anything. If you tell them that, the yelling and fighting will definitely start!" Andy semi-smiled, but his brow was wrinkled. "I'll wait in the car while you tell them."

"No," Jack, reconsidered, "I think I'll wait in the car - you tell them."

"It's your idea!"

"I'll write a message." Both were now smiling. "One of these days I'll write the message and mail it. Special Delivery."

"What about tonight, Jack?"

"Close your door. Lock it. Stuff cotton in your ears."

The next morning in the first round of the doubles, Andy was erratic and unsure. Rick backed him up and recovered points for most of his bad plays. He took charge and called out positions. The last three games Andy was right in there with him.

They won 6-3, 6-2.

In the semifinal round of the singles, Andy was playing tough against Bob Marlon. This time he was determined to beat him. Marlon was just as determined and edged Andy 6-4, 6-4.

Andy and Rick won the next two doubles matches and went to the final against Marlon and a boy named, Hal Steed. Steed was a player from California visiting Marlon's family. In the warm-up, Andy hit everything to Steed as hard as he could. The boy was slow-moving and couldn't hit as hard as Andy. It was a fairly even matching. The big difference was Andy and Rick tried harder.

Andy had confidence. His serve went in most of the time and he made some good plays at the net. Rick was cool, taking charge, directing the play, knowing Marlon's weakness, and hitting the ball at his feet.

At the Coke machine, Jack heard Brian greet Warren Trane. Jack turned and sure enough, it was Warren Trane, the tennis club manager. He was with one of his assistants.

"How's the tournament going?" Trane asked.

"No problems," Brian answered, confidently.

Trane looked at the board and draw sheets. He paused at the 14 boys' doubles. "I didn't know Rick Gordon was playing. Who's he with?"

"Andy Valdez. Plays here at the park."

Jack was nearby but Trane made no sign of recognition. Jack had no intention of speaking first.

Trane and assistant walked between the courts. Jack fell in behind them, close enough to catch every word. Trane stopped at the court where Andy and Rick were playing. Andy hit a hard forehand that won the point. Trane watched for about five minutes.

"The Gordon boy is coming along," Trane commented, and gestured to Andy. "That Valdez kid, plays here at the park?"

"Yeah. Been at the club tournaments a few times."

Trane shook his head, "Where did he learn to play so badly? Look at that swing. Terrible."

"Kids here don't get decent instructions, I guess."

"Terrible!" Trane repeated and walked back down the walk. He passed Jack without a glance.

Jack stared and said softly, "Damn snotty bastard! Who the hell does that crummy bastard think he is? Came down from the clouds to look at us common peasants. And, that's all he can say about Andy, 'Where'd he learn to play so badly?' What a damn crummy bastard you are, Warren Trane!"

Andy ran to the fence. "Hey, Jack! We won!"

"That's terrific!" Jack said, enthusiastically. He kept quiet about Warren Trane.

The presentation of the trophies was scheduled for two o'clock Saturday. The awards table was set up on the lawn near the green courts. The photographer from the Deseret News arrived in a station wagon. He was young and had a thick black mustache. He set up his equipment, carefully checking the distance and the background. He didn't like the background: the court's wire fence. He changed the angle and now it seemed satisfactory. The position of the sun was approved.

Andy watched with impatience. He had been waiting a long time, more than a year. A tournament player without a trophy is like a bullfighter without the ears, the fisherman without the fish on a plaque, the hunter without the antlered head on the wall.

Two matches were still in progress, the finals of the 21 mixed-doubles and the 18 girl's singles.

Doug Wixom and his partner, Lorna James, were ahead one set and 3-1 in the second. Jack watched. Doug tried blasting their opponents off the court to get it over with. At the fence, he asked Jack, "Hold them off, will you, Jack? I want to be in that picture. I'm trying to finish this."

"I'll ask," Jack said.

"I've never been in a picture," Doug whispered. "Might impress the coach."

"I'll see what I can do."

"Do it."

Jack went to the presentation group. The trophies were lined up on the table in three rows. The singles trophies were one inch taller than the doubles trophies. The winners were gathering. Relatives and friends stood nearby and everyone was smiling.

Jack found the tournament organizer, one of the father's from the tennis club. He told him the situation and asked if the ceremony could be delayed.

"I don't think so. Everyone has to get back to the office including the photographer. I'll stall as long as I can."

"Thanks, could be ten minutes - if they don't go to a third set."

The design of the trophies was modern and beautiful. Square ebony base, fluted column of gold rising up with a graceful figure of a tennis player reaching for the sky with his racquet. They were inscribed, Deseret News Public Parks Tennis Tournament, the division won and a place for the winner's name. Andy was anxious and could hardly wait. He went to the table and found his trophy - the one that belonged to him. He earned it and it was his - but not until he had it in his hands would he know for positive it really was his.

"Ladies and gentlemen," a tall man from the Parks Department said loudly, and everyone turned and listened. He thanked the sponsors, the people involved and the players. He talked about how wonderful the event was and that it inspired and encouraged young players.

Applause and smiles. He called out the names of the winners and awarded the trophies to the victorious.

"Rick Gordon and Andy Valdez. Boys fourteen doubles."

Andy and Rick stepped forward, "Congratulations."

"Thank you."

"Thank you."

Andy held his trophy tightly, like a treasure he would never give up.

Jack smiled and laughed, so happy it almost hurt.

Doug Wixom and his partner came running from the court. "We took it!" Doug announced, smiling. "Six-three, six-four."

The photographer lined the winners in three rows, the front row kneeling. Andy and Rick stood proudly in the second row. Andy held his trophy with both hands close to his chest and thought, cheese as Jack had told him. A flash.

"One more!"

Again, the victory smiles. Another flash.

It was over.

The next morning in the sports section, eight columns wide at the top of page two, was the picture of them all, with a banner line and a column-deep article.

Two weeks later in the shop Andy had a question for Jack. "I hope you haven't forgotten about my birthday." He was at the aquarium, feeding the fish.

"How's the tank?" Jack asked. "The corner leaking?" He was at the job press, getting a form lined up.

"I'll be thirteen. No, it's not leaking. Maybe a few drops. It's a little wet where you patched it."

"I hope it holds, don't want another flood. What a mess! Water and fish all over the floor."

Andy laughed, "That was funny, trying to find all the fish and get them in the bucket."

"Seems funny now."

"Did you hear what I said about my birthday?"

Jack took the form off the press, put it on the stone and unlocked it. Two small "w's" were missing. He searched through the forms on the back of the paper cutter.

"How do those fish look, any dead ones?"

"Five guppies, three neons, the gourami, the catfish, the beta and the two swordtails. None, all there. The new swordtail is sure pretty. But the beta is the best. He's the prettiest fish I've ever seen."

"I'll say," Jack agreed. "I've seen a lot of betas, but that's really the prettiest."

"I really don't know what I want for my birthday. I need a back tire for my bike and some new tennis shoes - a lot of things."

"Son of a gun! Can't find another W. Need one more. Andy, you've got to help me put this type away one of these days. Forms all over the place, and not enough type in the cases."

"Birthday's the seventeenth. Tuesday. Only two

weeks away. I'll be a teenager, you know?"

"Thirteen! Good gosh, how'd you get so old all of a sudden? Seems like you were only eleven a couple of months ago."

"That was a long time ago, Jack. I'm almost thirteen, the seventeenth, Jack. Tuesday."

"What the dickens do you want for your birthday?"

Andy hesitated, "I wish my dad could see me now. Maybe he would like me now."

Jack stopped what he was doing and stood straight up. Andy had never mentioned his father, only that his mother hated the father with a vengeance. "Andy," Jack started, thoughtfully, "he left for other reasons, not because he didn't like his kids. Who knows for sure why? Only he and your mom know the whole story. You had nothing to do with it, always remember that Andy. You had nothing to do with him leaving. Kids are the hostages when parents divorce. They get caught in the middle and have no say - usually they don't even know why it happened. Both parents have their own side. Don't blame yourself, you had no say. Someday, you'll understand, but for now . . . what can I get you?"

Andy felt emotion swelling his chest and tears in his eyes. He didn't want to cry. "I guess I need tennis shoes for my birthday present."

"When'd you say it was?" Jack was searching for another "W" again.

"The seventeenth. Tuesday."

"The seventeenth? Seems to me it was the twenty-sixth. Okay, so this year it's the seventeenth. If you want tennis shoes that's what you'll get. Sure beats me why a thirteen-year-old would want tennis shoes for his present, though. I can think of a hundred things I'd rather have."

"It isn't what I want . . . it's what I need. I've got to have them for tennis. You sure can be difficult at times."

"Here it is, found another W. If you look long enough around the shop, you'll find what you need."

"I need shoes, Jack."

"All right, Andy boy. Got the message. Want them wrapped with a blue ribbon?"

"Just a plain old brown paper sack will be fine."

"Go look in the stores and see if you can find some good Converse."

"I don't know how much it would cost."

"Here's a couple of dollars. See if that's enough. Anyhow, have them put them away and you can get them tomorrow."

"Is that all I get? A two-dollar present?"

"I had in mind a yellow MG or a red Corvette, but I guess I'll have to make do with shoes."

"Ah, Jack, you're always fooling." Andy laughed. "Be serious."

"I'd rather be Jack."

"Ah, Jack."

"Go see about those shoes before the stores close. When you get back we'll talk about your birthday. I think maybe you need a new tire for that bike or maybe something else. Okay?"

"Sure, Jack. That's just what I was telling you."

"I know, Andy, I know."

A few days later, Andy was playing doubles with Doug Wixom on number one court. He felt great. He was

189

playing well, keeping up with Doug and making some terrific shots. Their opponents, two students from USC, visiting Salt Lake City, were tough players, but Andy and Doug were staying ahead of them.

Doug made a fast serve. It was returned straight down the center, low over the net. Andy made a jump, reached, sliced it over the net and out of reach. The USC students couldn't touch it. Andy threw his racquet in the air, caught it and swaggered back to position for the next serve.

"Lucked out," Doug commented with a smile. Doug always played to win, a practice set was strictly a life or death matter.

Next serve out. The second in. Back to Doug. Return cross court to Andy at the net. Andy angled it to the corner. A hard volley to Doug. Returned down the center. A hard smash back to Andy's left. Somehow Andy got hold of it, backhanded down the center right between the players. Neither could get a piece of it.

Spectators lined the fence.

"Good play, Andy!" someone shouted.

"Who is that kid?"

"Andy Valdez."

The match ended in two sets. Andy and Doug taking it 6-4, 7-5.

It was 11:30 p.m. when they finally left the park. Jack was elated.

"Some show you put on," he said. "Some show."

"I was playing pretty good, wasn't I?"

"Pretty good! I'll say you were playing pretty good. You're not just a tennis player, you're a performer. You had everyone watching. I could have passed a hat around and picked up a few dollars. Next time you do that, I'll charge admission."

Andy blushed and laughed. "Didn't know I was putting on a show."

"I don't know what else to call it. You sure looked good out there. The bigger audience you have, the better you play. Why don't you do that at the club? Every time someone important is watching you freeze up. Damn, if Warren Trane could have seen you tonight. I wish you'd play that way at the club."

"I don't like playing at the club. Those people staring at me like I was something that crawled in. I feel like a raisin in a bowl of rice."

"I sure liked the way you played tonight. It was fun watching. You sure made Doug hustle to keep up. He really had to put out."

"It was a fun night," Andy swelled with pride.

Thursday night when Jack arrived to take Andy home, he came running up waving his racquet.

"Hey, Jack! Guess what?"

"All right, I give up."

"I get to try out for the Intermountain team. Mr. Wendell came down and told Brian he wanted to talk to me about it. So we talked and he said I should be on the Silver Flite team in the fourteens. The tryouts are tomorrow morning. He said I should make the team sure! But I have a play-off, so he can see whose best, and what position they'll play."

"Great. Real great. What time?"

"I forgot, I'll ask Brian." Andy ran to the clubhouse.

The boy's excitement made Jack feel good.

Brian came out, "Hi, Jack."

"Hey, Brian."

"It's ten o'clock at the University tennis courts. Know where?"

"I can find it. What's this Silver Flite thing?"

"It's for the unranked players. It's the team from the tennis club, only it's representing Salt Lake City."

"I'm going back and practice," Andy told them, excited. "Hey, Jack, Brian's got a special on balls. He's got old dead, stale balls for sale cheap." Andy laughed and ducked out the door, expecting Brian to throw something at him.

"What's the joke?"

Brian grinned and shrugged, "I've got some used tournament balls for twenty-five cents each. Good for practice."

"I've got a trunk full of practice balls. This team thing is a pretty good deal for him, huh?"

"First kid from the park they ever asked."

"Maybe he ought to have big letters on his shirt, Liberty Park Club."

"I don't think they'd like that."

"No, they wouldn't."

"These balls are almost like new, Jack. Real good buy. I'll make it five for a dollar."

Jack reached for his wallet. "Okay, Brian, okay."

Returning from the post office in the afternoon Friday, Jack passed the entrance to the Atlas Building, just as Arnold Thomas was coming out.

"Oh, Jack - I tried to call you. Did you know about Bert?"

"Is he still in the hospital?"

"He died this morning."

Jack stared at him. "I thought he was getting better."

"He was in pretty bad shape."

"Didn't know it was that bad."

"He went downhill this week, nothing they could do."

"I should have . . . should have gone up to see him."

"The funeral is Monday."

Jack nodded.

"I'll let you know the time."

"All right, Arnold. Let me know."

Jack went down the alley and into the shop. Sitting on a table was the letterhead for Bert's business, Jack hadn't run it off yet. There were times he liked Bert and times he didn't. He wasn't a very warm person, but he had always been kind and friendly. He recommended Jack's printing to friends in business. Still, Bert had been a friend for a long time. One of his first customers.

He sat down. He didn't feel like working. Remembrances flooded in. He should have gone to the hospital more often. It had been more than a week. You don't have many friends you can really depend on to help you, he thought to himself. When you need someone, its great to know you have someone you can call. Hell, I can count my honest-to-God real friends on one hand.

Jack turned off the lights and locked the door behind him. He went into the rug room and closed the door. Light from the stairway globe created long streaks on a wall and part of the ceiling. It was very quiet there, no steam pipes and the offices above were vacant.

In the dimness, he sat on a pile of rolled-up rugs. This was really away from the entire world. He could think and remember here. He laid down, using a rug for a pillow. A dull rumbling sounded from the alley as a heavy truck went by. Then dark silence. How could that happen to Bert? He lived so damn cleanly. Never drank. Never smoked. Probably never even been in a bar. Church every Sunday. Watched his health and food, never got overweight, exercised every day. What the hell did all that do for him?

The Christmas cards. Every Christmas, Bert bought two boxes of cards for him to imprint. From Mr. and Mrs. - until two years ago. Then, just Mr. He thought about all the times they had lunch - and dinner. Bert driving him around town when his car was down. The last time they had lunch. Bert ordered a hot beef sandwich.

"Just a little gravy," Bert told the waitress.

There had been too much gravy.

"Gravy kills me," Bert said.

"Don't eat it then."

"I don't know. I can't seem to eat anything. It cuts me up inside. I've got to go back to the hospital in a couple of weeks. Soon as I get more strength. I don't know what the hell they'll do then. They nearly cut out all my guts. I can't eat too much. I get hungry and can't keep it down."

"You'd better not eat that gravy."

Bert pushed some of it off the roast beef.

"You're looking good, Bert. You really are. You just need to put on some weight. You'll be fine."

"I'm trying . . . can't seem to keep anything down."

I should have gone up to the hospital more - and phoned. I really didn't know it was that bad. I could have talked to the doctor and found out how bad it was. What could I have done? Bert had a lot of hospital insurance and had the best doctors in town.

Jack knew damn well what he could have done. Bert didn't need a lot of visits or phone calls. Just one, to tell him what a good loyal friend and a nice guy he was. Jack was thankful for everything Bert had done for him.

"Oh damn, damn, damn, damn, damn." He hit the rug with his fist and cried.

In the tryout for the Silver Flite team, Andy won his first two matches, then lost the third. He was given the number two position in the singles matches. Then, the three day tournament began. The Silver Flite teams played at the University of Utah courts and Bob Wendell picked up the boys every morning and drove them to the courts. They defeated Idaho and Montana, losing only one doubles match. The final day was tough on Andy. Two singles matches in the morning, a doubles match in the afternoon. Back to the shop, he was so tired he nearly fell asleep in a chair.

"Go into the rug room," Jack told him. "Take a nap until I finish this job. We'll go eat and I'll take you home."

"Huh?" Andy answered, head nodding.

Jack said it again.

"Okay. I could sleep for a week. Tennis is sure hard work sometimes. It was hot up there today. Must have been a hundred and ten. I sure had to run to win. Anyhow, I get another trophy."

"You get an 'A' for Accomplishment, too. Get going - I'll wake you."

The next morning, for the individual matches, Jack picked up Andy at his house. His eyes were puffy - he had cried most of the night. His back was red and tender with welts from a belt whipping. Punishment for being gone all day and then mouthing off to Fred. Andy had talked his way into a beating, despite warnings from his sister and mother. Andy got home full of himself while every one else was walking on eggshells. No one wanted to hear about tennis or Andy's insistence that what he was doing was more important than staying home and cleaning the house.
He got out of bed at six, dressed quietly and waited outside until Jack arrived to take him to his other world.

"What's wrong? You look tired. I told you to get some rest! Look, if you're running around after I drop you off . . . that's no good, and makes me angry! You need to get some rest when you go home. This is an important tournament!"

"Don't worry Jack, I'm ready . . . I couldn't sleep last night."

"You look awful! Let's get you something to eat and some orange juice."

"Just get me out of here before they wake up. My mom gets mad when she thinks all I do is play tennis and not help around the house, she might make me stay home."

"Did she say you could go?"

"Yes - but sometimes she changes her mind without warning. Let's go."

"Okay, Andy - I don't want to get you in trouble."

"It's okay, Jack. But I'm real sore. My back is sunburned cuz I played without my shirt yesterday," he lied.

"Terrific! I told you not to do that. When are you going to listen to me? Now you'll be stiff and slow. You have to play through the pain, understand?"

"I will, Jack. I promise."

The singles matches were being played on new courts near some new two-story student housing. A golf course was across the road and sloping up from it the Wasatch Mountains. To the west, the wide, long valley spread out below them, bordered by the Oquirrh Mountain range. It was a pleasant sight on this cool August morning. To the northwest, the lake spread across the horizon and jets approached the Salt Lake Airport in the distant clear sky.

Several ladies from the tennis club keep the schedule running smoothly. They direct players to courts and answered the numerous questions from out-of-town players, some from far distances in Montana and unheard of towns in Idaho, Wyoming and Colorado.

Andy checked the schedule. "I play some kid from Pocatello."

"Take him good," Jack told him.

"Hey, Ken!" Andy greeted a friend. "You were in Idaho last summer. You know this kid, Harold Bend? I play him."

"Harold Bend? I think so. If I remember right, he's pretty good. Oh, sure, I remember. He was fourteen champ of Idaho last summer. I've got Joe Borden first round."

"Take him this time."

Ken grimaced. "Sure. Every tournament this year I've got him. He kills me."

"I've got to get to work," Jack told him. "Phone me

if you don't get a ride back. So play tough, both of you. See you later."

Andy defeated the boy from Idaho, 6-4, 7-5. He figured it made him Idaho Champ. He lost in the second round. With Larry Banning as his partner, he went to the semifinals in the doubles. It was a fine tournament.

September arrived and school started. Homework every evening and reports and compositions. Jack continually tried to convince Andy school must be taken seriously. Two months later, it was report card day.

"How come you get these remarks all the time?" Jack asked.

"I guess they don't like me."

"Liking you has nothing to do with it. Those teachers aren't there to like you. All the teacher wants from kids is no trouble. You don't make any trouble for them and get good grades, they're happy as the pigeons in the alley." He paused and read, "Look at these remarks: 'Andy has the capability to do better but doesn't apply himself as he should.' 'Gets up and walks around in class.' 'Doesn't work as hard as he should.' 'Should do much better in this class.' What is all this foolishness for?"

Andy shrugged. "I don't know - I get restless. Can't sit still a whole hour."

"The teachers say you're smart. Okay, we'll buy that. You've got brains, but they're rusty."

"Those teachers are always jumping on me for something. Anything goes wrong, it's my fault. Somebody throws something and the teacher yells at me."

"Why should she yell at you?"

"Don't know. She just doesn't like me."

"Look, don't give me a snow job. You've been throwing things so she just naturally figures it's you. Right?"

Andy thought about it and laughed, "Maybe."

"You've got to get better study habits, Andy. I mean it. Here you are in junior high and goofing off like it was forever. Look, you don't make good grades you'll just be out of luck going to college. You've got to have good grades to go to college. Right?"

"If you say so."

"I know so! They don't want no ignorant lazy kids who can't do the lessons. You've got to learn now to get good study habits. You make it a point every night to do your lessons. When you've got one of those projects that takes a lot of time and looking up things at the library, you get on it right away - not the very last damn day."

"You're always talking about me going to college. College this, college that. How am I going to college without a lot of money?"

"Ah, come on, Andy."

"Tennis, tennis, tennis."

"Right, right, right. You're going to the University of Utah. You're going to be on the tennis team. But first, you need to get better grades. And then you get even better grades in senior high. And, you'll practice, practice, practice tennis every chance there is. You'll be number one at West High. Believe me. They've got a sorry team at West. When you get there, you'll stir things up all right."

Andy looked up at him and half smiled. "I don't know if I want to go to college or not. I could get a job in a market and buy a car. College is just four more years study-ing. I hate studying and stupid teachers yelling at me. I get the blame for everything. Anybody does something, first thing they do is yell, 'Andy, you stop that!' or 'Andy, go to the office!'

"The principal has a special chair for me in his office. He says, 'Andy, I'm sorry to see you here again. You've spoiled my day.'"

"I believe it."

"You're always sticking up for the teachers."

"I'm just telling you what's right for you. The teach-ers have got hundreds of kids to worry about. You're just another kid, another problem. Kids come and go. A teacher can't keep track of all the kids, so she wants no trouble. She wants you to get your lessons finished and behave in class. Then, the teacher thinks you're real great. Okay?"

"Well . . . "

"Say yes, okay."

"Yes, okay."

"All right. You don't go to school for the benefit of the teachers. The school was built at great expenses for you. You're the only reason they've got a job - to help you be somebody. Get a good education and learn how to grow up and be somebody useful. You've got to have a good educa-tion to get a good job. You've got to have a good job to make good money. You've got to have money to do the things you want to do and buy the things you want to buy."

"You're always talking about money like it was such a big thing."

"I don't make the rules. I'm just telling you the rules of this world. Without money you're a dog - a real dog in this world.

"Look, money isn't everything but if you want to have some security and have a good job and a good car and money in the bank, and have people treat you with respect you better get an education. Believe me, from personal experience. Make something out of yourself. Be somebody. You're smart. You've got personality. Believe it, most people really like you. Man, what I wouldn't have given to have had the chances you have now. Andy, you can do anything in this world you want. You can be anything. You can really be somebody."

Andy was smiling, glowing. "You make it sound real great."

"It's all there for you. You just have to want it real bad. There's a saying by the Spanish, 'In this life take what you want. But pay for it.' You get the point?"

Andy sighed, "Yeah, I get the point. I can have anything I want, but first I have to do my lessons and get along with the teachers."

Jack snapped his fingers. "Amazing. Already, you understand. I thought I would have to tell you every day. Now it's all settled. No more problems and no more weird notes on the next report card and no more visits to the principal's office."

"I didn't promise all that!"

"I know. But you'll try."

"Yeah, I'll try. Is there anything to eat around this place?"

Good luck seldom comes in quantities. Bad times settle in and never wants to leave. October overwhelmed

Jack like a plague, starting with a letter from the paper company.

"Your account has been past due for several months. You have made little decrease in the balance in this time. We regret that drastic action must be taken. Unless paid in full within ten days, we will be forced to turn this over to our attorney for legal collection."

Jack phoned the paper company manager. The explanations were not considered satisfactory; the promises of payment made no impression. He had ten days - or else. He put away the phone, the solution was somewhere but right now he couldn't find it. He decided he would think about it tomorrow.

The next day a letter from the Internal Revenue Service arrived. He needed to get down to their office immediately and explain his income tax payment. He hadn't yet figured out what to do about the paper bill and now he had income taxes. He gathered up all his receipts and notes and scribblings - everything he could find. He knew they cared little about his figures and receipts, all they wanted was money. He had plenty of figures and receipts, but not the elusive money.

Low cold-looking gray clouds hovered below the peaks of the mountains like a thick ocean fog. A north wind shivered him. Winter was inevitably coming, too soon again. The federal building, a massive chunk of gray granite, with holes chiseled out for windows and doors, stood before him. Up the elevator to the third floor; he was in no hurry. Three other taxpayers were in the elevator with him, two carried large envelopes, and the third carried a bulging brief case. They looked as worried and as unhappy as Jack.

A dumpy woman with careless clothes and a bargain shop wig waited at the counter. She gave him the kind of look one might give an ex-con who had broken parole and was now in for it - but good. She found a fat folder and looked through it. There seemed to be a lot of paperwork concerning Jack Keller.

"Mr. Keller, I see you're habitually delinquent. Last year was late, and the year before, and the year before that. We can't put up with this any longer."

She had a voice a crow might be proud of. It hurt Jack's ears.

"I will try . . ."

She quickly interrupted, "We are not going to listen to any more excuses. The department is cracking down on delinquent payers. You have exactly one week to get this balance due in this office. And in full. No partial payments. If you do not, we'll take steps to confiscate your property!"

Her voice had risen to a shriek; and it was painful to Jack. He could imagine this ungraceful female screaming commands at boot camp.

"You have one week! We expect you to return with the full payment. If not, we will have to take immediate action to get our money! You understand?"

He turned and hurried away. What could he say to this hair-pie? In the hallway, he stopped and leaned against the wall, afraid he was going to be sick. He had a sudden, sharp headache. Confiscate his property. Take his print shop. He would prefer to welcome Armageddon. Let there be firestorm and tornado and earthquake and endless rain and all the land burst and be destroyed and drowned. And, that dreadful woman lanced and struck down by vipers and eaten by jackals.

Out of the building, going down the steps, the clouds opened and let rip an explosion of vicious rain. The streets and sidewalks were flooded almost immediately. Everyone scurried for shelter. By the time he reached the car, he was soaked. The motor wouldn't start and the wipers didn't work.

A white flare of lightening lighted the sky overhead, and then a blast of thunder shook the little car.

"Oh, for God's sake!" Jack cried out, then he laughed. He laughed so hard tears came. Another flash in the sky and a hammering thunder. Jack shook his fist. Somebody up there was sure laughing at him.

A few days later, a letter arrived from the landlord. Inside, a long itemized statement showing a balance of $648.45 rent due. A note was included: "This amount must be paid in full within one week or we will be forced to take drastic action. Due to increased expenses, beginning the first of the month, your rent will be increased $15 per month. Please attend to this matter immediately."

He showed the message to Andy.

"What does it mean?"

"It means we have to get out of here."

"We have to close up the shop?"

"We don't, they will. We don't seem to have any choice, Andy."

"What are we going to do with all the stuff?"

"Well. We'd better take what we need most. The equipment maybe I can sell and pay off the bills. I don't know, Andy. I sure put a lot of time and money in this place and it all ends up as nothing. It's like I made a rope and now it's going to hang me."

"Jack, we can't leave. It's like a second home to me. I like it here. Where will I go?"

"I've had some good days. And a lot of bad ones. I guess I got started all wrong. Not enough money in the first place. Not enough good equipment. Too much debt. All the time the expenses go up. The taxes, the phone, the paper and ink - every other thing. Now the rent. A guy like me shouldn't even try to make it by himself."

"I sure hate to leave this shop, Jack. What are you going to do now? Working, I mean?"

"Oh, I guess I can get a job in some shop in town. I'll call around. I don't know. Maybe now's the time for me to go to Los Angeles. I could get work there easy enough."

"Don't go now, Jack. I need you to help me in school and with tennis. I'd never be able to get in the tournaments if you weren't here to help me."

"I didn't know this would happen so quick. Seems like everything hitting me at once. Like, at last I'm paying for all the mistakes I've made. Well, if all the mistakes I've made in my life have to be paid for now, all at one time, I've sure got some bad days ahead. You'd better not come around for awhile. Trouble and bad luck can be contagious."

"I don't care, Jack. I'll stick with you no matter how bad things get. You just don't go to Los Angeles and I'll help you work things out. You'll get a good job, and all the bills will be paid, and everything will work out all right. You'll see."

"We'd better figure out what we want in this place and get it out of here while we can."

"There's the fish and my rock collection and my

comic books and I've got a lot of clothes here."

"You've got more stuff here than you have at home."

"This is my home, Jack."

Making things more difficult was the Fall Tournament at the club. It was held this year in October instead of September. Andy needed this tournament to help him in the rankings. He was sure to get ranked in the four-teens for the state. Singles or doubles, perhaps both. So, he had to be in this tournament.

When they went up to the club for the second round of the singles, Jack was not in a pleasant mood. It was the last tournament of the year again, and the long winter lay ahead. Andy needed to play through the winter but Jack was no closer to getting Andy in the club than this time last year. He counted on having the hundred dollars membership fee but it was not to be. The Internal Revenue had taken every cent and he still owed $20 more. There was the paper bill and the rent, too.

Jack had a quarrel steaming up inside and only need-ed someone to hang it on good. He hung it on Warren Trane. Andy was playing on court 2 below the balcony. Trane was watching the matches. Jack asked him his opinion of Andy's ability. Trane wasn't impressed.

"He needs good competition and lessons," Jack told him. "All he knows is what he's picked up at the park."

"Does he have an application in to join the club?" Trane asked.

"He hasn't got the money."

"We've got a waiting list a yard long."

"You haven't got a kid waiting as good as he is."

"We've got plenty of kids here who are better."

"They already belong. Show me one kid waiting to join who is better than Andy. You get him here and have a playoff. Winner gets a membership. That's fair."

"We don't happen to run the club that way, Mr. Keller."

"How do you run this club, Mr. Trane? You have to be rich and lily white, and live on the right side of town? Is that it, Trane?"

"Don't talk to me that way!"

"You're making me talk to you that way! What the hell kind of sport is this? A boy has to have rich parents to play? He hasn't a chance unless he's got rich parents. Is that the kind of game you have here, Trane? It isn't really ability, is it? Just the money - and which side of town you live on - and who you know. And, maybe how you spell your name."

"That's all, Mr. Keller! I've got other things to do!"

"You listen to me, Trane! I want something settled right now. I want that boy a membership some way, and you better figure out how he's going to get it. He can work for it, but he's going to get it."

"Get the hell out of here, Keller! Nobody tells me how to run this club!"

"It's about time someone did! Maybe for once you can do something for a west side kid who wants to be a tennis champ more than anything else in the world. You and the USLTA have done nothing to encourage him and hundreds of boys like him. Add it all up and it amounts to a big zero! An absolute nothing. A kid doesn't have to be rich to play Little League baseball or football or basketball or any other sport. But this damn game that you aristocrats sponsor is about as democratic as sheep in a lion's cage."

Trane went into his office and slammed the door.

Jack followed and pounded on the door.

"Don't run away and hide, Trane! You can't close the door all the time! The door's got to open sometime. Someday, you'll have to open the door, Trane!"

The room was filled with club members - boys, girls, men and women watching and listening. Disapproval was plain on their faces. Jack now noticed them. There was an angry murmur, like the buzz of a hornet's nest. Jack turned and faced them. Suddenly, he realized how outnumbered he was.

The outburst against Trane cleared his mind and spent his bitter emotions. He looked at all the people staring at him, not too close to him, but waiting for someone to give the signal to lash out at him in retaliation for having made an attack against their leader.

He wanted to laugh. There he stood like the lone unarmed man, his back to the corral fence, facing the angry mob waving a long new rope, pointing to a nearby tree.

Mr. Walsh cleared his throat, "Ah - I don't think Trane wants to talk to you. Really."

"I'm sure he doesn't," Jack replied.

"It would be better if you left."

"I'm sure it would." He made no move to leave. There was a silence for some seconds. He wanted to see what they were going to do.

Walsh cleared his throat, "I, ah . . . "

Jack saw Carla Banning in a corner, standing away from the crowd. She held up her right hand and gave him the peace sign and smiled. Jack smiled back. If anyone touched him, he was going to bust them and break them apart. He wanted to show Carla he wasn't afraid of anyone. He wanted to laugh. My God, this was ridiculous!

Walsh attempted a stern glare. Somehow, it didn't come off. Jack ignored him and just stood there waiting.

"I think we'd all better get back to our tournament," Carla Banning spoke up.

There was a murmur of relieved approval. Smiles and bright conversation started - all ignoring Jack - and then everyone filed out, leaving Jack and Carla there alone. Andy stood in the doorway, a questioning look on his face.

Carla laughed, "I think you've made your point."

"Have I?"

"I'm sure you have."

"With Trane?"

"Jack, things will work out."

"I hope they can."

"Jack, Jack!" Andy said, excited, "I won!"

Jack laughed, then became emotional, "Good for you," he sobbed. "Good for you kid."

Ten days later on a Saturday morning, Jack drove to Andy's to get him to help move things they wanted out of the print shop. When they arrived at the shop, an extra lock was on the door. A very large solid steel lock that looked like it could have secured a bank vault. There was a note: Please come to the office about this matter.

"What do we do now?" Andy asked.

"Any thing in there we really need?" Jack said.

"Just the whole place."

"I don't know. This could be the best thing in the world that ever happened to us."

"I don't see how. It was like I lived here."

"It was like I lived here, too. Sometimes, you think it's a bad thing happening to you. Then later, maybe, it turns out good. You never know. You just have to wait and see how things turn out."

"We could take the hinges off and open the door."

"We could. But we won't. I called Joe Barnes at Sunset Press last night. He's got a job for me. I don't think much of the idea of working for someone else, but there'll be a payday every Friday."

"What'll I do now?"

"You can come up town after school. Meet me at the shop. Joe's all right. Maybe you can make some deliveries. Earn a little money. Things will work out, Andy. I won't go to Los Angeles this year. I'll see you keep going with your tennis. Anyhow, I've gotten used to having you around."

"You need someone to bawl out and scream at once in a while, too, Jack."

"Yeah, right."

"What'll we do now, Jack?"

"Let's go down to the Jade and have an egg foo yong sandwich. You can play the pinball machine and I'll read the paper. Later, if we can find a dry court, you can practice. Have to get ready for next summer, Andy. There are lots of tournaments to be won next year."

He took a last look at the shop. The orange and green striped awning above the door that his wife made. She had been very good seamstress and it was a neat looking awning - as good as any you could buy. He hadn't let himself think about it for a long time. She had been very good at a lot of things. She could cook like a dream. And she knew how to love a man. There was no use going into all that. It had ended and forever it would be ended.

The shop and all the life he has spent there was now ended, too. And there was nothing he could take with him for all those years but the memories and the blue and yellow sign on the door: JACK KELLER PRINTING. He had been happy and proud when he put up the sign. He was going to have the best print shop in Salt Lake City. Someday.

On the bulletin board hung the samples of his printing. They were good. No one in town could have done better. The auto dealer letterhead, the candy company folder, the sporting goods business card. To Jack they were works of art, his creations; out of his mind and fashioned with his hands. He wished he had somehow done things differently. At that moment, he didn't know exactly how he could have. From day one, the whole project was probably headed for this inevitable day. Standing there outside the shop, the massive lock on the door shutting him out, and now day one had become day zero.

"Well, Andy, say goodbye to it."

"Goodbye everything," Andy said.

They left the building for the last time.

PART THREE

The psychologist's office at the V.A. Hospital was a floor above admissions, where Andy left Jack that morning. Jack's behavior had deteriorated in the few months since Andy found him at Smith's Food King. Jack would often get angry and insulting at night. He took off, regardless of the time, making his way downtown, before Andy would find him. Andy searched all hours of the night, sometimes receiving a call from the police after they found his business card and telephone number in Jack's pocket.

It was a struggle keeping Jack clean or even dressed appropriately. He once found his way to the Courthouse looking for Andy, dressed in a woman's blouse and pants that were falling off. During the day, he was passive, but at night he became agitated and seemed delusional.

The psychologist seated at the desk was the only sign of life in the small office. The walls were bare. A metal desk and two chairs the only furniture. He stared at Andy for a few seconds before speaking.

"I know you . . . well some of my colleagues do. They testified in some case. You were defending some guy . . . a murder case."

"Oh, how did I do?"

"According to them and what I read, you were a take no prisoners lawyer. You've been in the paper a lot, too. Now you are a judge, right?"

"I've been very lucky."

"What is your relationship with Mr. Keller?"

"Jack Keller helped me when I was a boy. He took me off the streets. He was a life saver."

"I was wondering what the connection could possibly be," the psychologist wondered out loud.

"He's my friend. He cared for me when I needed someone, and now I'm trying to take care of him. He has nobody."

"Well, he's lucky to have you! We examined Mr. Keller psychologically and gave him a physical as well. Your friend has onset Alzheimer. He has some dementia and delusions. His delusions are frequent and the gap is closing. As you know, he can't take care of himself. Given his age, eighty-years-old, Jack will need assisted care twenty-four-hours a day."

"What does that mean?"

"Hopefully, it means a nursing home for now."

"Jack won't stay, he takes off. I think he hallucinates, too. He'll walk out the door."

"Eventually, Jack will need to be housed in a unit for Alzheimer's residents, or maybe a psychiatric unit. The delusions increase at dusk and nightfall. He has what is called, Sundowner's Syndrome. When the sun sets, there is a chemical reaction in Mr. Keller's brain that throws him off balance and he is more prone to delusional thinking and dementia. If he is wandering off, it is only a matter of time before he will be victimized or hurt."

"He already has been. According to Jack, some kids took the money I gave him and assaulted him. It happened a few nights ago," Andy reported.

"That's too bad. I can refer you to a few places that closely watch and monitor residents. Some have locked units for residents who shouldn't leave without assistance."

"Where is he now?"

"We admitted him. He is in the Forensic Unit for more testing and clinical intervention. He will be here for about a week. In the interim, you can check some referrals for bed space and services, if you would like." The psychologist handed Andy a sheet of paper. "Here's a list, some are marked for veterans only."

"Thank you, doctor, but I have concerns about where you have Jack. I'm familiar with the Forensic Unit, I used to visit clients there. It is the psych ward. The place is full of vets with mental disorders. They are allowed to walk the halls and they assault staff and patients. It is very dangerous, you have Jack in a shark tank. He is an old man . . . he's eighty! I've been trying to protect him from the streets and now he is in a building full of drugged-out mental cases. I don't think so, I'll take him home."

"Judge Valdez, you are a good friend. You've done all you can for Jack. He is where he needs to be. Especially with his age and problems. Don't worry, he will be in our diagnostic and evaluation unit, separated from the resident population. We will watch and protect him. You can visit him anytime. He won't be able to leave and we can do more assessments and help find a place for him to live when he is discharged," assured the psychologist.

"You're probably right doctor. I don't want him here long term. I mean, as a long term resident."

"He won't be. You do need to accept the fact that you won't be able to care for him. He needs twenty-four-seven care, professional care."

"Can I see him tonight?"

"Yes, I'll give you directions and get you clearance. Be aware that Jack is probably medicated and it's nightfall, which may make for a short visit. He may be out of it, reality wise."

"Thank you doctor, for your patience and help."

"No problem, good luck."

The visit did not go well. Jack saw he and Andy's reflection in the window and went berserk. He finally calmed down after Andy closed the blinds and assured him that no one was at the window trying to kill him. He laid down and fell asleep quickly.

Andy left with mixed feelings. He was relieved that help was on its way, but saddened too, knowing that from now until Jack died, he would be living in a building, probably locked in.

Oh well, beats the streets, Andy said to himself. He remembered those were the exact words Jack said to him when he took him from the streets and into to the shop. From the shop and then to the tennis courts, almost forty years earlier.

Hope was happening then and now, Andy concluded as he drove home. As he passed Liberty Park tears streamed down his face.

EPILOGUE

Jack Keller died four years later in a nursing home in Logan, Utah. Jack described living at the Sunshine Terrace Alzheimer's unit, "like living in a Country Club. I get twenty-four hour care."

Over time, Jack's memory faded and he no longer recognized Andy during visits. On fleeting occasions, he did remember that Andy was a judge. He bragged to the nurses. Sometimes, out of nowhere, he would ask Andy if was playing at Wimbledon, or ask him how he was doing on the professional tennis tour. Andy would go along with Jack, trying to squeeze their shared life and passion to the last spoken word between them. Ultimately, Jack would phase-out and shut down completely, only breathing and staring vacantly, oblivious to Andy's presence.

At the end of Jack's life, the friendship and care between this man and the boy had come full circle. Their chance meetings, when Andy was a boy, then again almost forty years later, graced their lives with hope and the feeling that they mattered. Sometimes, hope happens without even knowing it.

Jack D. Keller

My good friend, mentor and guardian angel, Jack Dudley Keller, passed away peacefully at the Sunshine Terrace Nursing Home, Logan, Utah on April 17, 2000.

Born May 31, 1916 in Pittburg, Kansas, son of Jack H. Ward and Ellen Torgerson. His father died when Jack was two years old and he was later adopted by his stepfather, Silas V. Keller, the father of his only sister, Irene Keller. His mother, sister, and stepfather, all preceded Jack in death.

Jack, or as he liked to be called, "Jack Mormon", was raised early on in coal mining towns such as Price, UT in his youth settling in Salt Lake City where his mother operated a boarding house during the Great Depression. Jack was a West High graduate, member of the tennis team, and Red and Black school newspaper staff, always a Panther.

During World War II, Jack served his country stationed in the Aleutian Islands for which he wrote and told many stories to me and others.

Jack is not survived by any biological children other than the many "poor west side kids" he helped throughout his life. Specifically, Judge Andrew A. Valdez, who he "discovered" when Andy was a young boy "on the street hustling" as a paper boy for the Deseret News. He taught and guided him throughout his life. Their close friendship and father/son relationship continued until Jack's passing this past week.

Thank you Jack for treating me special and showing me the way. Thank you for teaching me how to play tennis, reading the New Yorker, New York Times, Cervantes, and Somerset Maughn. You were right! — My education saved my life -- I am forever indebted to you. How lucky we all have been that even though you called yourself a "Jack Mormon" you practiced the teachings of the Savior. God Bless You.

Jack desired to be cremated and was buried at his mother's graveside, Salt Lake City Cemetery on April 28, 2000. An interment dedication will be held at the Salt Lake City Cemetery Saturday, May 6th, 10 a.m.

Printed in the United States
212348BV00001B/4/P